N

M 27
A 3051
A 32
A 3
River Itchen
Hamble River
A 335
SOUTHAMPTON
A 27
Botley
River Meon
Netley
Hamble
Warsash
Sarisbury
Titchfield
A 27
M 27
A 27
wood
den
Hythe
Fawley
Calshot
SOUTHAMPTON WATER
FAREHAM
Portchester
Portsmouth
A 32
A 275
PORTSEA
ISLAND
HAYLING
ISLAND
Beaulieu River
Exbury
Calshot Spit
Lee-on-the-Solent
GOSPORT
rd
Lepe
Needs Oar Point
THE SOLENT
Alverstoke
Southsea
PORTSMOUTH
THE
COWES
East Cowes
Osborne
House
SPITHEAD
RYDE
Newtown Bay
A 3020
River Medina
A 3021
A 3054
B 3330
Newtown
A 3054
Carisbrooke
B 3401
Newport
FORELAND
Calbourne
B 3323
ISLE
OF
WIGHT
A 3056
SANDOWN
B 3399
A 3020
SHANKLIN
A 3055
B 3327
VENTNOR

TS

ST CATHERINE'S POINT

Based upon the Ordnance Survey ¼" map with the permission of the Controller of Her Majesty's Stationery Office. Crown Copyright Reserved.

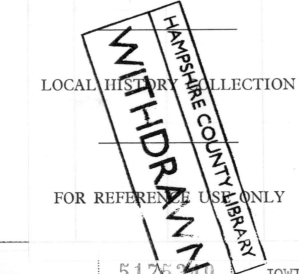

THE SOLENT AND ITS SURROUNDINGS

THE SOLENT AND ITS SURROUNDINGS

by

R. L. P. and Dorothy M. Jowitt

TERENCE DALTON LIMITED

LAVENHAM . SUFFOLK

1978

Published by
TERENCE DALTON LIMITED
LAVENHAM   .   SUFFOLK

ISBN 0 900963 88 3

All photographs, except where stated,
by Robert E. Jowitt

Text Photoset in 11/12pt. Baskerville

Printed in Great Britain at
THE LAVENHAM PRESS LIMITED
LAVENHAM   .   SUFFOLK

Contents

Index of Illustrations

* * * * * * * *

To Lucinda Jane, with love

Introduction

HOW astonished the first inhabitants of the Solent area would be if they could see it now! To the modern mind, the name "Solent" brings a vision of sails: yachts and boats of all sizes, designs and descriptions, with sails, white or of brilliant colours, throng these waters at every summer week-end, forming a delightful picture against the background of the Isle of Wight. The earliest inhabitants, however, were probably there long before sails were thought of at least in this part of the world. Boats were not so necessary, because what is now the island was part of the mainland, and the Solent only a river, fordable in several places.

As recently, by geological reckoning, as a quarter of a million years ago, the Needles formed part of a chalk ridge, joining on to the Old Harry Rocks, near Swanage, now divided from them by about fifteen miles of sea. The source of the Solent was, it is believed, in what is now Somerset, and as the river flowed south-eastward, other rivers from Gloucestershire and Devonshire flowed into it. After passing through what is now Poole Harbour, it was joined by the Dorset Stour and Hampshire Avon, whence it flowed on through what are now known as the Solent and Spithead, and finally out into the Channel south of where Brighton now stands. Freshwater fossils from this time are still found in the Isle of Wight.

It is not known exactly when the sea broke through. Geologists and historians are rightly cautious of assigning dates: probably it was a gradual process taking thousands of years. There are some fossil and skeleton evidences of prehistoric life in the district. After the last Ice Age, this part of Great Britain was the first to become habitable, and human life has existed here for several thousands of years. Those early inhabitants must indeed have been surprised if they could have seen not only the sailing ships, but the car-carrying ferries, the cruising liners and the vast oil-tankers, while the hovercraft and hydrofoils, and the helicopters and other planes, must have seemed like something positively devilish.

Even the modern inhabitants and visitors sometimes find the noise extremely trying but, apart from this one disadvantage the Solent is ideal, with every imaginable land and water sport for holiday-makers, and accommodation to suit every pocket. The fascinating historical towns and villages along its shores, and only a few miles away inland the glorious scenery of the New Forest to the north, and the varying charms of the Isle of Wight to the south, make it an area of inexhaustible delight. It is also admirably suited to industry, with its excellent communications by land, sea and air, but people who dislike industrial areas can very easily escape from them into the peace and quiet of the sea-shore and the countryside, or can imagine themselves back in the historical or even prehistorical past.

From Southampton, there are daily services to the continent and, indeed, to the whole world, but people who cannot afford to travel need not be downhearted, since they can find almost everything they want in this little section of the British Isles.

This book is planned as a round trip, east to west from Portsmouth to Poole along the north shore of the Solent, across to the Needles, and west to east along the south, or Isle of Wight, shore to Ryde, including inland places of interest within easy reach of both shores. During this round trip all buildings mentioned are as they were at the time of writing.

R. L. P. and Dorothy M. Jowitt,
New Milton,
Hampshire.
July, 1978.

CHAPTER ONE

Portsmouth

T HOUGH old maps of the Solent show it extending eastward only to Cowes in the Isle of Wight, and to the eastern shore of Southampton Water in Hampshire, newer maps make no clear distinction between the Solent and Spithead, and Portsmouth appears to be washed by the shores of both. As one of Great Britain's most historic cities, it makes a good start for a tour of the Solent area.

Known familiarly as "Pompey" to the British Navy, of which it is the headquarters, the greater part of it occupies Portsea Island, which is about four miles long and two miles broad. A small settlement grew up in late Norman times round a creek known as the Camber, at the south-west corner of the island. This settlement became important enough to be granted a charter by Richard I in 1194, and a church, now the oldest part of Portsmouth Cathedral, was built a few years earlier.

Portsmouth had been an important naval base and home of the King's fleet for years before Henry VIII built the first naval dock in Britain there in 1540. The Royal Navy gunnery training establishment, H.M.S. *Excellent*, torpedo establishment, H.M.S. *Vernon* and the submarine headquarters, H.M.S. *Dolphin* are all at Portsmouth as is the Royal Naval Hospital, Haslar. This well known hospital takes its name from a creek in Portsmouth Harbour, was founded in 1746 and designed by John Turner. It was, when completed, the largest naval hospital in the world and the largest brick built building in Europe.

Portsmouth was vulnerable to the French, who attacked and burnt it two or three times in the fourteenth century. Early in that century, Portsmouth was guarded by one man-at-arms and two archers, and their very arduous duties were supposed to be eased by the construction of defences known as Long Curtain Battery, consisting of ramparts and a moat, ending at the east with what was then called the Greene Bulwark, but altered in George II's time to the King's Bastion. These defences still stand, near what is now Clarence Pier. They proved, however, quite inadequate, and early in the fifteenth century a strong Round Tower was built near the harbour entrance, and a little later a wooden tower was built at Gosport opposite this. The Saluting Platform and the Square Tower (c. 1494) were added, and these defences also remain. Henry VII and Henry VIII both enlarged the docks, as well as

The bows of H.M.S. *Victory*.

extending the fortifications. Across the harbour mouth there was what the historian Leland described as a "mighty chayne of Yron", said to have cost £40. This chain was renewed from time to time, and it is interesting to note that, when Samuel Pepys wished to have it renewed about 1664, there were for a time not enough men available to do the work because the plague was raging. Another of Henry VIII's defences was Southsea Castle, one of a chain of forts which he ordered to be built along the south coast from Kent to Cornwall. He was unpopular in the Roman Catholic countries, because of his divorce from Queen Katharine of Aragon, and he anticipated a joint French-Spanish invasion. The castle had a square keep and a dry moat. It was different in design from most of Henry's other castles, being built with straight lines and sharp angles: the others had round keeps and rounded bastions, but the angled bastions, of which Southsea Castle may have been the first example in England, were found to be better suited to the guns of that date. Although the castle has been much added to and altered, some of the Tudor walls and gunports remain. Not long after its completion, the castle guns were used in an action against a French fleet which approached round the eastern tip of the Isle of Wight. This action came to very little: partly because of these guns and partly due to the considerably increased strength of Henry's Navy. The French very soon withdrew but the main casualty of the English fleet on that July day in 1545 was the *Mary Rose* which was swamped through her lower deck ports and sank rapidly. Her captain, Sir George Carew and most of the 400 or so crew members were lost. Henry himself saw this event and was greatly distressed.* The defences were further improved during the remainder of the Tudor period, but no further action took place.

King Charles I was in Portsmouth in 1623, returning from Spain, where he had been in an unsuccessful search for a wife. As a thank-offering for his safe return, he later presented to Portsmouth a bust of himself by Hubrecht le Sueur. This is to be seen on the north face of the Square Tower, and under it is the inscription "After his travels through all France into Spain, and having passed very many dangers both by sea and land, he arrived here the fifth day of October, 1623". In 1625 he married Henrietta Maria of France.

George Villiers, Duke of Buckingham, a favourite first of James I and then of Charles I, but very unpopular with almost everyone else, was assassinated in 1628 outside a house, still well preserved, known as the *Spotted Dog* in the High Street. As Lord High Admiral, he had made various unsuccessful expeditions, and the last, a failure to relieve French Protestants beseiged at La Rochelle, added to his unpopularity. He was killed by a discontented officer, Felton, who became quite a popular hero, but who was nevertheless hanged at Tyburn, and his remains gibbetted on Southsea Common.

*There is hope that the *Mary Rose* may be salvaged.

During the Civil War, Portsmouth at first declared for the King. The Square Tower had been made into a powder magazine, and the Royalist leader, Colonel Goring, held this for some time against the Parliamentary forces and, when obliged to surrender, threatened to blow it up unless he were granted honourable terms. As this would have destroyed much of the town too, his terms were granted. Southsea Castle also fell to the Parliamentarians, and the whole town was obliged to surrender.

In 1662, King Charles II went to Portsmouth to meet his future Queen, Katharine of Braganza. They were married in the governor's house, which had formerly been the "Domus Dei", a hospital for "Christ's Poor" founded in the early thirteenth century by Peter de Rupibus, Bishop of Winchester. When it was made into the governor's house after Henry VIII's suppression of the monasteries, the chapel of the hospital was made into the Garrison Church. It was severely damaged in the air raids of 1940, but a part of it is still used for services. In 1670, Charles II called in Sir Bernard de Gomme, a Dutchman, who had been appointed "Engineer in Chief of the King's Castles in England and Wales" to improve the defences. He reconstructed them completely, bringing them up-to-date and embodying all the latest ideas on fortifications. They included the 18-gun battery at Portsmouth Point, near the Round Tower.

The dockyard continued to increase in importance and size. Its area had been eight acres in early Tudor times: William III reclaimed ten acres of mud-lands, and more docks were added from time to time. The modern dockyard covers over three hundred acres.

Portsmouth Cathedral stands at the south end of the old High Street, not far from the old Square Tower. The chancel of the beautiful twelfth century Early English church remains but, in the late seventeenth century, what had been the nave was rebuilt in the Classical style. This is now a part of the chancel, and a new nave was added c. 1930 to the design of Sir Charles Nicholson. A new west end may yet be built. The dome surmounting the tower is a prominent feature of the "Pompey" skyline and there is a ship weather-vane, nearly 7 feet long. The most notable monument is that of George Villiers, Duke of Buckingham. The church became a cathedral, and Portsmouth a City with a Lord Mayor, in 1926.

A Portsmouth character to whom millions of people have cause to be grateful was Jonas Hanway, born in 1712. While others were protecting the town against possible foreign attacks, he was protecting everyone from the rain, by pioneering the use of the umbrella in England. At the time he was much ridiculed, but who, now, would be without the umbrella, both literal and figurative? He also did excellent social work among the poor boys of Portsmouth.

3

Portsmouth Cathedral, with the chimneys of the power station in the background. These are prominent sea-marks.

4

The old High Street had many handsome old buildings, but many of them were destroyed in the heavy air raids of 1940, among them the old *George Inn*, where Nelson spent his last night in England. The Landport Gate, an interesting building believed to have been designed by Hawksmoor, stands at the far end of the street, and is now the last remaining gate of the old town in its original position.

The Dockyard lies to the north of the old town and is entered by a gate at the Hard. There are some good houses both on the way to, and in, the dockyard, worth noting when visiting H.M.S. *Victory* which, with St Ann's Church, is open to the public. This very typical Georgian church was much damaged in the bombardment, but has been well restored, and has some striking modern stained glass. The *Victory* was launched at Chatham in 1765, and, after being in several famous actions, and then going through various vicissitudes, was chosen by Nelson as his flagship in 1803. The glorious but yet tragic events of 1805 are too well known to need description. The *Victory* had a few more years at sea, and was then moored in Portsmouth Harbour, where she lay at anchor for one hundred and ten years. In 1824 she became Flagship of the Portsmouth Command, an honour which she still bears. In 1922 she was moved into No. 2 dock, the site of the oldest dry dock in the world. A careful restoration by the Society for Nautical Research followed, and she is now exactly as she was at Trafalgar.

On the other side of the road, opposite the *Victory*, is the Victory Museum, where there is a most interesting collection of figure-heads and other nautical relics, and the magnificent panorama of the Battle of Trafalgar by the late W. L. Wyllie, R.A.

As well as the *Victory*, there are two other monuments to Nelson. One is a statue in Pembroke Square, and the other a column on the top of Portsdown Hill, 300 feet above sea level and 150 feet high, with a bust of Nelson at the top. Although he died over one hundred and seventy years ago he, like Churchill, will always be remembered as one of the outstanding saviours of his country. Nelson was not only a national, or even an international, hero: he was also greatly beloved by all his men. After one of his voyages from Portsmouth, to Newfoundland and back in the *Albemarle*, every member of the ship's company volunteered to sail with him again. In general this was a time of brutal discipline in the Navy, with horrible food, and pay never raised since the time of Charles II, so very few captains found such willing crews. In 1797 the Mutiny at Spithead took place, and Nelson's efforts in explaining the men's grievances were instrumental in procuring an Act of Parliament to improve conditions. He sailed from Portsmouth before the Battle of Copenhagen as well as before Trafalgar, and on every occasion men were delighted to serve under him.

Among the naval officers of Nelson's time there were two of Jane Austen's brothers, and she must sometimes have visited Portsmouth with them. To her admirers the ramparts of Portsmouth are indelibly associated with the Price family, and Fanny Price's visit to their terribly sordid home, and its contrast with the refinement of Mansfield Park. Every Sunday morning the family attended the Garrison Chapel, and then walked on the ramparts for an hour or two, this being poor, harassed Mrs Price's one pleasure of the week. It was sometimes slightly marred for her by meeting her "trollopy-looking maid-servant" (as Jane rather surprisingly describes her) Rebecca, also taking a Sunday outing, with a flower in her hat. However, Mrs Price liked meeting her friends, who also enjoyed this promenade, and discussing the servant problem with them. The ramparts, and the dockyard with all its activity at that date, are most vividly described. Although Jane Austen lived for most of her life in Hampshire, *Mansfield Park* is the only novel concerned in any way with her native county, but the half-dozen chapters on Portsmouth are as good as anything in her writing.

To the north of the dockyard is Portsea, which had fortifications to protect both town and dockyard, quite separate from those surrounding old Portsmouth. By 1875, however, these were thought obsolete, and levelled, and some of their sites made into recreation grounds. The Unicorn Gate, which formerly stood at the end of North Street is a very handsome structure dating from 1778. It was moved in 1865 to its present site, on a corner of Unicorn Road and Flathouse Road, where it forms another entrance to the dockyard. The Roman Catholic Cathedral, St John the Evangelist, in Edinburgh Road, was begun in 1877, and is an imposing building of red brick, with Portland stone facings, in the Gothic style. The handsome church of St Mary, Portsea, was built in 1887-9 to the design of Sir A. W. Blomfield, the cost being contributed largely by Mr W. H. Smith, son of the founder of the famous firm of newsagents and booksellers. He himself vastly increased the firm, and became in due course an M.P., First Lord of the Treasury, and First Lord of the Admiralty. In St Mary's churchyard is a memorial to Admiral Kempenfeldt and the 800 men of the *Royal George*, who perished suddenly, without warning, in 1782, in an accident reminiscent of that to the *Mary Rose* two centuries earlier.

Another Portsea church, St George's, is a copybook example of a Georgian church, dating from the mid-eighteenth century. In the Reading Room belonging to this church, Charles Dickens gave some of his famous readings of his own works. He is one of Portsmouth's most distinguished natives, having been born at what is now 393 Commercial Road, on 7th February 1812. The house is now owned by the Corporation and is a Dickens Museum. Portsmouth does not feature largely in Dickens' novels, but it will be remembered that Nicholas Nickleby and Smike went there with Vincent

Crummles' theatrical company, which included the remarkable "Infant Phenonemon". Another famous native was I. K. Brunel, the celebrated engineer, who laid out the Great Western Railway and built several well-known ships. The fathers of both Dickens and Brunel happened to be working in the dockyard when their sons were born. Other distinguished authors connected with Portsmouth, though not all natives, were Sir Arthur Conan Doyle, H. G. Wells, Rudyard Kipling and George Meredith.

The work of defending Portsmouth went on through the centuries. Fort Cumberland, begun about 1745 and named after William, Duke of Cumberland, is a typical example of an eighteenth century "star-plan" fort, built at the south-east extremity of the island to command the entrance to Langstone Harbour. It is still in use by the services, and not open to the public. In 1851, when Louis Napoleon made himself Emperor of the French by a coup d'état, and called himself Napoleon III, there was another scare of a French invasion, and a Royal Commission recommended an ambitious scheme of fortification. Six large forts were built on the top of Portsdown Hill, some facing inland to guard against possible attack from the landward side. The possible invasion did not take place, and these forts were not of much use at the time, and were scoffed at and called "Pam's Folly", Palmerston being then Prime Minister. There were five small forts to guard the Gosport approaches and, most remarkable of all, four forts standing up in the sea off Spithead. From the ramparts of Southsea Castle, which is now a museum of Portsmouth history, open to the public, there is an extensive view of all these forts, which form a "ring fortress", unique in Britain.

Spit Sand Fort, which stands in the sea off Southsea front, is one of four built to guard Spithead in the invasion scare of 1851.

None of these defences were of much use in the devastating air raids of 1940, when the Guildhall, among other buildings, was almost completely destroyed. It had been an excellent example of Victorian Classical, built 1886-90 by Cuthbert Brodrick. It has been restored by E. Berry Webber, in much the same style but without its former cupola. The Portsdown Hill forts were in use during the preparations for D. Day in 1944, and the Allied Supreme Headquarters, Advance Command Post, was at Southwick only a few miles away. One of the forts is now a radar station, one a storage depot, and others have been taken over by the Portsmouth Corporation and are open to the public.

Southsea, the seaside resort of Portsmouth, was only a wild common until the mid-nineteenth century, but, with its good sea-front, its charming views across Spithead to the low wooded shores of the Isle of Wight, and the short sea-trip across to Ryde, it was an obvious place for development. Hotels and boarding-houses were built in vast numbers, and beautiful public gardens laid out. Every possible kind of indoor and outdoor occupation, sport and entertainment has been introduced, and of late years special stretches of water have been reserved for the exciting modern sport of water-skiing. The climate is mild, and Southsea prides itself on having almost a record number of "sunshine hours". There are also the Navy Days, when modern fighting ships can be visited, and the *Victory* is dressed overall in honour of her present-day successors. With historic Portsmouth and modern Southsea combined, it is difficult to imagine a better holiday resort, at least for those who love the company of their fellow-humans.

Besides play, work is well represented. Thousands of people are employed in the Naval Dockyard, and industries in Portsmouth and nearby include boat-building, aircraft-building, engineering, machinery and machine-tools, metal-work of various kinds, electrical industries, building and allied trades and, to provide refreshment when the work has been done, breweries.

Just beyond the Solent area, eastward, are Hayling Island, with safe, sandy beaches for children, and Langstone Harbour and Chichester Harbour, both noted for sailing. Chichester Harbour branches off into several fascinating little creeks, on which are some delightful old villages, including Bosham. This has a very good Saxon church, and a daughter of King Canute is buried in the churchyard. There is a picture of this church in the Bayeux Tapestry, as Harold is believed to have set sail for Normandy from Bosham. Chichester is a charming old walled city, with its beautiful cathedral, its famous modern theatre and, just outside, the wonderfully-restored Roman Palace at Fishbourne. It is very easily reached from Portsmouth and Southsea, and should certainly be included in any visit to the area.

The Portsmouth Football Club has played in the Football Association Challenge Cup Final three times; it lost by two goals to nil against Bolton Wanderers in 1929, by two goals to one against Manchester City in 1934 and won the cup in 1939 by beating Wolverhampton Wanderers by four goals to one.

Since 14th October 1975 broadcasts have been made from the Independent Local Radio Station at Portsmouth, Radio Victory. This commercial station serves the greater part of the Solent and the Isle of Wight.

The Royal Yacht *Britannia* and the Trinity House vessel *Patricia* dressed overall for the Naval Review, 1977. Portsdown can be seen beyond the waters of Portsmouth Harbour.

CHAPTER TWO

Portchester, Fareham, Titchfield

HUNDREDS of years before there was any settlement at Portsmouth, Portchester Castle was built on a peninsula jutting out into Portsmouth Harbour. It was the westernmost of the chain of forts erected by the Romans to defend the south-east coast of Britain, during the latter part of the third century A.D., as a bulwark against raids by Saxon invaders. The coast here was a part of that known as the "Saxon Shore" and an official, known as "The Count of the Saxon Shore" was responsible for its defence. The *Notitia Dignitatum* is a list of officials of the Roman Empire, and from this we learn that the Roman name of Portchester was probably *Portus Adurni*? In 284 the Emperor Diocletian appointed Carausius, a Belgian seaman of humble origin, to command the Roman fleet in the channel, using Boulogne as his headquarters. Carausius, having revolted against Diocletian, set himself up as an independent Emperor, and for seven years "ruled the waves", but was finally murdered by Allectus, one of his officers. Allectus then reigned for three years, but was himself then defeated by the Emperor Constantius Chlorus, who restored Britain to the Roman rule.

(Quite a different account of these events relates that Carausius himself built the fort as a defence against the Roman forces, who were anxious to re-conquer Britain.)

The walls of the fortress are still wonderfully perfect, and date from the last quarter of the third century A.D. They are 18 feet high, and enclose 9 acres in a nearly perfect square. Fourteen of the original twenty bastions remain. The castle is built of flint with bonding courses of brick. It had gateways in the centre of each side, the more important gates in the east and west sides and posterns in the north and south. Further defensive measures consisted of a system of V-shaped ditches, double on the landward side but single elsewhere. A bank and ditch which cuts across the neck of the peninsula, and which had been considered prehistoric, have now been proved to be medieval. Extensive excavations in the outer ward, under the able direction of Professor Barry Cunliffe, have yielded much valuable new knowledge.

After the departure of the Romans in the early fifth century, the castle was re-occupied from time to time by the Saxons, who no longer came as raiders, but as peaceful folk. According to the *Anglo-Saxon Chronicle* there was an early sixth century occupation. There is also some evidence that, during the eighth and ninth centuries, ploughing was carried on, some timber buildings constructed and storage and cess pits dug. In the twelfth century, the old Roman fortress was converted into a medieval fortress, one of three or four great Royal castles on the south coast. A strong keep was built in the north-west corner of the old fort, in the first half of the twelfth century. It was heightened in the early thirteenth century, so that it could command the entire fortress. It is still intact. The Roman gateways were replaced by new ones, easier to defend.

In 1133 a monastery of Augustinian Canons was established by Henry I, but their residence here lasted only about fifteen years. They occupied the south-east corner of the old Roman fort but, finding the surroundings of the castle too noisy for their liking, they retired to Southwick, a village beyond Portsdown Hill. All that remains of the monastery are the chutes of the rere-dorter (sanitary convenience) high up on the Roman wall.

During the thirteenth and fourteenth centuries the castle became a royal embarkation point for the many wars against France. It was visited by several monarchs, notably Henry I, John, Henry II and Edward II. The neighbouring Forest of Bere was ideal ground for hunting, always an important consideration with the medieval kings.

The church is late Norman of the finest type, and owes its preservation to the fact that it was both a monastic and a parochial church. The rich Norman door in the west front leads into the austere, aisleless nave. The church was formerly cruciform, but the south transept has been demolished. The magnificent font, carved with men, beasts, birds and reptiles, is of a type found in some churches in Northumberland. There is a monument to Sir Thomas Cornwallis (1618) who had been Groom-Porter to Queen Elizabeth I. It takes the form of an alabaster demi-figure in armour. There are two displays of the Royal Arms, commemorating Elizabeth I and Anne, the latter example being extremely handsome.

The magnificent Roman walls of Portchester Castle.

11

During the twelfth century, the castle was used both as a treasury and a state prison. The Bishop of Glasgow, captured during a war against Scotland, was held there in irons.

Edward III stayed at Portchester in 1346, while waiting to start on yet another war with France, which culminated in the magnificent victory of Crecy. Richard II left his mark on the castle, and ordered a completely new palace to be built. This was, in fact, constructed during the years 1396-9, but he did not live to see it, having met a tragic and mysterious death at Pontefract Castle in Yorkshire. The interior of Portchester palace is now largely in ruins, but the exterior remains. A flight of steps led up from the courtyard to the Great Hall, a fine building lit by three two-light windows. South of this was the kitchen. The Great Chamber occupies most of the west range and this is a very magnificent hall lit by four fine windows. It was to have been the king's living-room and place of private audience, and opening out of it was the king's bedroom.

On the opposite side of the courtyard is the east range, at the north end of which is Assheton's Tower. Sir Robert Assheton was Resident Constable from 1376-1381 and he built the tower which still bears his name. Henry V stayed at Portchester while he fitted out the ships that were to take part in the expedition which led to the victory over the French at Agincourt (1415). Soon after this, the rising port of Portsmouth began to supplant the old Roman fort, and in 1441 the castle was described as "ruinous and feeble" and its only use seems to have been as a military store. Henry VIII paid a visit to the castle and ordered a large naval store-house to be erected. Elizabeth I also visited Portchester towards the end of her long reign. During the many wars of the eighteenth century the castle became a depot for the confinement of prisoners of war. Special floors were inserted in the keep for their accommodation, and many prisoners cut their names on the walls.

In Victorian times, during the Crimean War, Portchester Castle was seriously considered as a suitable place to build a vast military hospital, but fortunately the suggestion came to nothing, the hospital being built at Netley. In 1926 the Castle was placed under the protection of H.M. Office of Works, now the Department of the Environment.

Portchester Lake is one of the creeks of Portsmouth Harbour, and there is a yacht yard quite near the Castle, with various facilities for yachtsmen, though the approach is rather difficult. There are one or two sailing clubs, as there are in most of the Solent creeks.

Portsmouth, Portchester and Fareham now form an almost unbroken stretch of built-up land, but about one hundred and fifty years ago, according to Cobbett in his *Rural Rides*, the lower slopes of Portsdown Hill and the land to the south of it were good corn-growing country, the wheat being of particularly excellent quality. Agriculture and horticulture still flourish in the district quite near the built-up areas: the soil is good near the Solent coast, and there is usually plenty of sunshine. There are some farms, and market-gardens abound in the Fareham district.

Although Fareham is largely a modern town, with a very modern shopping centre, its history goes back into the very far past. Human habitation there seems to date from prehistoric times, paleolithic and mesolithic flints having been found in gravel beds. There are some indications that shell-fish collecting was an occupation there in the mesolithic period. In recent excavations, Roman pottery and other relics of the first to fourth centuries A.D. have been discovered, and Fareham was a likely place for the Romans to have had a settlement, as there was a good fresh water supply from a river. There is also evidence of Anglo-Saxon habitation. The parish church has some Saxon work. At the time of the Domesday Survey, the Bishop of Winchester held a large estate at Fareham, and in 1296 another Bishop of Winchester had to pay considerable sums for the defence of the sea-coast there from raiders. In 1306 the town returned two members to Parliament, and through the centuries it was a flourishing market town and quite an important port. It had a good trade in timber, pottery, bricks, flour, high-quality leather, chalk and other goods, produced in and around the town and exported from there.

At that time there was a good channel down to Portchester and Portsmouth, and ship-building and sail-making were other important industries. These are still carrried on to a lesser extent, and Fareham is still a small port with some coastal trade, but the channel is no longer so good. In spite of this, Fareham is a popular yachting centre. Fareham Lake, or Fareham Creek, is the north-westerly part of Portsmouth Harbour, and lesser creeks running from it have such interesting names as Bombketch Lake, Spider Lake and Crabtree Lake. There are several quays and hards, and the usual clubs. Yachtsmen need considerable skill, as there are mudbanks and other hazards. The creek is navigable up to the old bridge in the town, but at low tide there is very little water. Fareham has one beautiful street, the old High Street, in which nearly all the houses are Georgian, many with bow-windows. The parish church, St Peter and St Paul, which stands at the north end of the street, at the corner of Osborne Road, is of many dates. There is Saxon "long-and-short" work on the north-east corner of what was formerly the Early English Chancel, now the north chapel of a newer chancel, designed by Sir Arthur Blomfield in the early 1880s. In the north aisle there is a fourteenth or fifteenth century oak reredos. The brick tower, with a cupola, is eighteenth century, and the nave, which had been destroyed and rebuilt in 1812, was rebuilt again, to the design of Sir Charles Nicholson, in the early 1930s.

Holy Trinity Church, in the middle of what is now the shopping centre, dates from 1834-37. It has a good stained-glass west window with figures of Faith, Hope and Charity, similar to those by Reynolds at New College, Oxford, some interesting monuments, including two by Flaxman, and some very good modern interior decoration by S. E. Dykes Bower. There are also two interesting modern churches of the early 1960s, St Columba, Highlands Road, and St John the Evangelist, Redlands Lane.

Bishopwood, the residence of the Anglican Bishop of Portsmouth, lies at the west end of Fareham. It is a fascinating building of the "Gothick" type, has a thatched roof, and must be unique among Bishops' Palaces.

Titchfield Abbey.

About 2½ miles west of Fareham is Titchfield. Titchfield Abbey was a house of Premonstratensian Canons, the name being derived from the monastery of Prémontré in France. They wore white robes, and were known as White Canons to distinguish them from the Benedictines, who wore black. The House, which was founded by Peter des Roches, Bishop of Winchester, in 1232, passed a peaceful existence for three hundred years. During this period several Royal visits took place, including that of Richard II and Anne of Bohemia, and Henry V on his way to Agincourt. It is believed that Henry VI was married in the abbey church, by Bishop Ayscough of Salisbury, in 1445, to Margaret of Anjou, to whom he had already been married by proxy before she set sail for England. This strange custom was quite usual in those days.

In 1537, however, the abbey shared the fate of many others, and had to surrender to Henry VIII's Commissioners. The abbot was awarded a pension of £66. 13. 4.; eight of the canons £6. 13. 4., and three novices £5 each. These were reasonable sums at that date. One wonders how these monks fared on returning to the world, which they thought that they had left. Thomas Wriothesley, later Earl of Southampton, who was Thomas Cromwell's principal agent in the dissolution of the monasteries, began the work of partially destroying the abbey buildings and converting what remained into a fine house for his own use. He demolished everything east of the crossing, including the central tower, choir and transepts. He also built a most imposing gateway right across the middle of the nave. This occupied the south range of the former cloister court. There are some grotesques on the string-course beneath the parapet, but one lady wears a "pedimental" cap. Other graffiti on walls include a sixteenth century ship and a gibbet. The great doors still remain.

From south to north are the west wall of the vanished north transept. Next comes the entrance to the library and then the entrance to the chapter house or meeting place of the monks. This, though blocked, is quite complete and is good thirteenth century work, with Purbeck marble shafts. Just here are the graves of the first two abbots, Richard and Isaac. The north range contained the monks' frater (dining hall) which became Wriothesley's dining hall. Just beyond is the entrance to the monks' dorter (dormitory). The walks of the cloister court are paved with medieval tiles, of the late thirteenth or early fourteenth century. They were saved at the Dissolution and are of great interest: some are floral or geometric, and some heraldic. At the entrance to the frater there is a somewhat mutilated inscription in Latin, with each tile bearing a letter. This may be freely translated, "When you sit down to a meal, remember the poor".

The mansion, which had some very fine red brick chimneys, was re-named "Place House". Fortunately for Wriothesley, he managed to retain the favour of the king at the time when Thomas Cromwell had lost it and been executed. Wriothesley was made Secretary of State, and later he was created Baron Titchfield, became Lord Chancellor, and was made Earl of Southampton as a reward for his services in connection with Henry's divorce.

In 1547 Henry died, and was succeeded by Edward VI. Wriothesley was a member of the Council which, on account of Edward's youth, had been established to rule with him, but he lost the favour of Protector Somerset, who drove him from office and fined him heavily. However, like many other prominent people in this stormy period, Somerset himself in due course went to the execution block, while Wriothesley remained alive to witness the event. He died in 1550, aged forty-five, and was succeeded by his son Henry, second Earl of Southampton, who entertained both Edward VI and Elizabeth I at

Place House. The third Earl, another Henry, was imprisoned because he secretly married one of Queen Elizabeth's ladies-in-waiting, Elizabeth Vernon, and later, in 1601, he was imprisoned again, in the Tower, on suspicion of having been concerned, with the Earl of Essex, in a conspiracy. There is a story that a beloved cat of Wriothesley's managed to go to him down a chimney, and to keep him company in his imprisonment. He forfeited his estates, but regained them all, and was completely restored to favour, on the accession of James I. He is chiefly remembered now as Shakespeare's patron. "Venus and Adonis", "The Rape of Lucrece" and probably many of the sonnets, are dedicated to him, and there is some slight evidence that some of the plays, possibly including "Romeo and Juliet", may have been performed at Titchfield.

There were many royal visitors to Titchfield Abbey and Place House, partly because the situation, near the tidal creek of Fareham, was convenient for monarchs visiting Portsmouth. Charles I and Henrietta Maria paid a visit there in 1625, and in 1647 he was there in very unhappy circumstances, having fled there from Hampton Court during the Civil War. From Place House he was taken to Carisbrooke in the Isle of Wight by Colonel Hammond, the Parliamentary Governor, who, Charles wrongly thought, would be persuaded to come over to his side.

Place House was occupied until about 1781. By this time the Wriothesley family had ceased to possess it, and later owners dismantled it and used much of the stone for the construction of Cams Hall near Fareham. One of the owners was the Duke of Portland, and the heir to this dukedom still takes the title of Marquis of Titchfield.

Approaching Titchfield village from the south.

Titchfield is a charming little town, with many comfortable-looking eighteenth century houses in its broad High Street. It is situated in a wide valley, quite unspoilt although there is suburban development quite near on either side. The church is of great interest. The west entrance is by a seventh century Saxon door, said to be the oldest piece of ecclesiastical architecture in Hampshire. Saxon quoins may also be noticed at the south-west corner of the south aisle. The lower part of the west tower was a Saxon porch, from which a beautiful late Norman doorway leads into the nave. The very fine monument commemorating the second Earl of Southampton and his parents is in the south chapel. There are three recumbent effigies by Gerard Johnson, a refugee from religious persecution in Flanders (1594). The tomb is of marble and alabaster, in the Renaissance style, with large obelisks at each corner. On the south wall of this chapel is a pathetic tomb, possibly the work of Epiphanius Evesham, to Lady Mary Wriothesley, who died in 1615 aged four. There are several other very interesting tombs and tablets, including one on the north wall to the Hornby family (1836), with a recumbent female figure by Chantrey, and on the west wall there is a large painting of "The Miraculous Draft of Fishes", commemorating the Reverend W. M. Cosser, Curate and Vicar, 1843-87.

The monument to the Earl of Southampton in Titchfield Church.

CHAPTER THREE

Gosport and the Eastern Shore of the Solent

FROM Fareham, there are two ways of approaching Gosport, one to sail down Portsmouth harbour, and the other, far less pleasant, to go by the A32 road. On the way from Fareham is the suburb of Rowner and Bridgemary. Rowner lies just off the A32, to the west. It was formerly a pretty little village, and still retains some of its charm and a few pretty old cottages, although it is now included in the borough of Gosport. It is mentioned in the Domesday Survey and the *Anglo-Saxon Chronicle*, and was visited by King Henry I in 1114 and by Edward I in 1277. It was associated with the le Brun, Brune and Prideax-Brune families, many of whose memorials are in the church and churchyard. One of the most beautiful is the tomb of Sir John Brune, 1559, in the chancel. Part of the church, including the present Lady Chapel, dates from the late twelfth or early thirteenth century, though much of it has been enlarged and restored. In the eighteenth century, this church was much used for the weddings of sailors stationed at Gosport and Portsmouth. Fort Rowner, one of the Palmerston forts, is in service occupation, and lies nearer the main road.

Formerly one could go from Fareham to Gosport by rail. One of the Gosport stations, dated 1841, was a very fine building with a magnificent

The ruins of Gosport Station; nearly as good as Ancient Rome.

colonnade, designed by the well-known architect Sir William Tite. Great efforts have been made to preserve at least parts of this station, but its future is uncertain. In the early railway days, Gosport station served Portsmouth also, and there was a floating bridge ferry, where there is now only a ferry for pedestrians, but Portsmouth had its own railway and station a few years later. Another station, where the Victualling Yard is now, was frequently used by Queen Victoria before she embarked in the Royal Yacht on her journeys to the Isle of Wight.

The name Gosport is said to derive from "God's Port", so named by Bishop Henri de Blois of Winchester when he, or some writers say his brother Stephen, sheltered there from a fearful storm in the Channel, c. 1140. Another possible derivation is "Gorse Port", from great quantities of gorse which grew all round the district, but the "God's Port" theory is more attractive, and it is known that Bishop de Blois granted two annual fairs to the village. For many centuries it was a quiet fishing village, but it was fortified in the Middle Ages with moated ramparts, now unfortunately largely destroyed, though a few small sections remain among modern developments. Defences were developed at various times, according to the requirements of the particular period. In general, the defences of Portsmouth and Gosport were complementary, but at the sad time of the Civil War Portsmouth, temporarily held by the Royalists, was attacked by Parliamentary forces from Gosport. The "mightye chaine of Yron" previously mentioned, joined the defences of Portsmouth to those of Gosport, stretching from near the Round Tower at Portsmouth to Blockhouse Point at Gosport. Forts were built all round the town of Gosport, Fort Blockhouse, at the nearest point to Portsmouth and just at the entrance to the harbour, being the most strategically placed. This was partly the work of de Gomme, who also built Fort Charles and Fort James. Some of the forts, having been found to have little strategic value under modern conditions, have been demolished, but some have been retained as service establishments of various kinds.

In the early nineteenth century, Gosport had an unenviable reputation as the scene of great depredations by the press gang, as many as five hundred men being captured by the gang on one night, and taken across to the naval ships at Portsmouth, but later, when the Royal Clarence Victualling Yard and other Naval, and more recently Fleet Air Arm, establishments were set up at Gosport, the Navy and the town came to be on very friendly terms. There was a smaller Victualling Yard in earlier days, with the rather sinister name of "Weevil Yard".

Weevil Creek and Lane still exist but not, one hopes, the horrible ships' biscuits and disgusting meat conjured up by the name. The Yard contains some interesting early and mid-nineteenth century buildings.

A small shipyard for building merchant ships was set up in Gosport in the late eighteenth century. Now there are many more shipyards, and Gosport is world-famous as a centre of the yacht-building industry. Hundreds of yachts of all sizes and designs are built there every year, many for export. Among famous yachts built there have been several contestants for the America Cup, and *Gipsy Moth IV* in which Sir Francis Chichester made his remarkable solo voyage round the world. Marine engineering and allied industries occupy a large part of the town, and along the water-front there are great tower-blocks of flats, but a few bits of old Gosport are still to be seen. In the High Street there are some pleasant old houses, and not far away is Holy Trinity Church, built originally c. 1696, as a chapel of ease to Alverstoke. It was enlarged in the eighteenth and early nineteenth centuries, and again, by Blomfield, in 1887, with a campanile added by him in 1889. Inside, it has two particularly interesting features. In the nave, which is original, there are two rows of Ionic columns made from oak trunks, and there is an organ, said to have been bought for a very small sum, on which Handel often played. It belonged to a patron of his, the Duke of Chandos, of Canon's Park, Middlesex, to whom he was organist. It was built under Handel's supervision, and he is known to have used it when composing "Acis and Galatea" and other works: possibly parts of "The Messiah" may have been tried out on it.

Another very interesting building is Haslar Royal Naval Hospital, a large, handsome, colonnaded structure built in the reign of George II, and externally much the same now as it was then, though naturally modified and improved internally. It has some good stone sculpture and a Royal Arms on the central pediment.

The Crescent at Alverstoke.

Alverstoke, now a residential part of Gosport, was formerly quite a separate village, and its church, St Mary, is the mother-church of Gosport. Bishop Henri de Blois is said to have founded a church there, but the present church was only begun in 1865, by Henry Woodyer, and its tower was added in 1906. The middle of Alverstoke still looks like a village, and there are also several good Georgian and Regency houses, including a beautiful crescent, very well restored. Bay House, Alverstoke, was built by Decimus Burton, c. 1840, for Lord Ashburton. It later became Gosport Grammar School and is now Bay House Comprehensive.

The coast between Lee-on-Solent and Stokes Bay, with the old *Queen Mary* heading out to sea.

Stokes Bay, west of Alverstoke and facing south-west, is the seaside resort part of Gosport, with the usual amusements, including a sailing club.

Lee-on-Solent, north-west of Stokes Bay, is another seaside resort within the borough of Gosport, with a small area of country between it and the main town. It is mainly a pleasant residential area and shopping centre, and has its sailing club, with its share of racing and regattas, good bathing and water-skiing. It also has an airfield, and the Fleet Air Arm School of Air Engineering and one or two other service establishments.

THE SOLENT

About opposite Lee, the waters of the Solent mingle with those of Southampton Water, that fascinating stretch of water, about ten miles long and two miles wide, running south-eastward from Southampton to the Solent, and fed by the rivers Test, Itchen, Hamble and Meon. This must be one of the most interesting shipping-lanes in the world. What Portsmouth is to the Navy, Southampton is to commercial shipping, and every sort of vessel, from huge tankers to tiny tugs, and from ocean liners to the smallest sailing dinghies, can be seen in this busy stretch of water. Formerly there were very pretty views of wooded country either way across Southampton Water, but now the view from the eastern shore is rather marred by the industrial development on the western shore.

The next place up the eastern shore from Lee-on-Solent is Hill Head, a large residential village. Just beyond this is Titchfield Haven, a small harbour at the mouth of the Meon River. This can be used by small yachts and dinghies when the tide is fairly high, but there are difficult sand and shingle bars, and at low tide the Haven is barely approachable except by local yachtsmen who know exactly where to go. The Haven is much frequented by birds as well as by yachts. Many varieties of wild-fowl, including Whooper Swans, inhabit it during the winter months, and it is also the home of interesting plants and insects. The Hampshire County Council has made it into a Statutory Local Nature Reserve, so that the wild life may not be too much interfered with by human life.

On the beach at Titchfield Haven.

About three miles further up Southampton Water is one of the most famous of all yachting centres, the Hamble River. During the summer months, the river is almost entirely occupied by yachts, from its mouth up to the village of Bursledon, two or three miles inland. Several well-known yacht-clubs have their headquarters there, and there is every possible facility for yachtsmen except, sometimes, mooring or anchoring space. There are so many local yachtsmen that it is as necessary for visitors to find out beforehand about accommodation as it is for landsmen to reserve at hotels. Formerly the Hamble River was noted mainly for crab-fishing; the yachting has grown up in the twentieth century. Near the mouth of the river on the east side, at Warsash, is the School of Navigation, with some good modern buildings: there are also some pleasant houses and gardens.

The Royal Thames Yacht Club was formed in 1775 as the "Cumberland Fleet". Following George IV's coronation commemoration regatta in 1823 a violent disagreement led to a breakaway group forming the Thames Yacht Club which was later granted the right to add the Royal prefix. Today the club, the oldest in Britain, has club-houses in London and at Warsash.

Opposite, on the west bank, is Hamble, an extremely busy centre for yachting and yacht-building, but also in part a very charming old village. There are some rows of early nineteenth century cottages, and some good Georgian houses and inns, and one or two from an earlier date. Sydney Lodge, 1789-98, a handsome house built by Sir John Soane, is now used as offices. There is an old rope-walk, and the main street of the village winds picturesquely up a hill.

Hamble Church, St Andrew, originally founded in the early twelfth century, still has several Norman features, doorways, windows and arches, some of them with zigzag and other carving, some good thirteenth century lancet windows, and an east window with fine geometrical tracery. The monuments are mainly wall-tablets, and include one to Sir Edwin Alliott Verdon-Roe, one of the pioneers of British flying.

In the more modern part of Hamble are the Air Training College and aircraft factories, and a little further up the west bank of the river the Naval Training College, and opposite this there is a pretty, wooded bit of country. Altogether, the Hamble River and its surroundings are a fascinating mixture of old and new, urban and rural, sea, land and air activities.

It is thought to have been much used by marauding Danes in earlier times. In early medieval times there was a small Benedictine Priory, of which practically nothing remains. This had an interesting exchange system with the monks of St Swithun's, Winchester. In return for some food, drink and clothes from Winchester, Hamble supplied 20,000 oysters every Lent, rather a curious example of Lenten fare by modern standards.

The River Hamble below Bursledon bridge.

At Bursledon, a little further up the west bank, warships were built in the seventeenth and eighteenth centuries. Now yachts are built there, and it has a regatta. Brick-making has been an industry there and at Lower Swanwick, opposite. The church, St Leonard's, is mainly late nineteenth century, by Sedding, but it has some interesting old monuments, including one to Philemon Ewer, shipbuilder, 1794, with a relief of a man-of-war and, on the outside wall, one to John Taylor, 1691, with a brickmaker's tool. There is also a Roman Catholic Chapel, Our Lady of the Rosary, c. 1906, with some fascinating, mainly Baroque, features. There are a few pleasant old houses, including the eighteenth century *Jolly Sailor Inn* by the riverside. Swanwick also has a few pleasing old houses.

Above Bursledon the river runs through country again, some of it wooded and very pretty, to Botley. Between Curdridge and Botley there is a Victorian mansion and park, Fairthorne Manor, formerly used as a training centre for boys going into the Merchant Navy. It is now run by the Y.M.C.A. as a camp where children and young people can learn sailing and canoeing and other outdoor activities, and an international camp for teenagers is held there every summer.

Botley is a large village or small town, with a market charter dating from 1267. It has some good Georgian houses and a few of an earlier date, an old mill, a town hall on pillars, and two churches. One, St Bartholomew, consists only of a thirteenth century chancel with a twelfth century doorway. The other, All Saints, is nineteenth century, but includes a twelfth century font and one or two other features from the old church. As Botley can be approached by small dinghies at high tide, it may be considered as connected with the Solent. William Cobbett, that aggressive, opinionated and rather self-satisfied, but at the same time amusing, courageous and very lovable Radical, had a farm there from about 1806 to 1826. It was from Botley, in 1810, that he was sent to prison for two years, and fined £2,000, because he ventured to protest strongly against savage sentences of flogging in the militia.

He was a hero to the people of Botley, who gave him a tremendous welcome on his return. There is a memorial stone to him, near the bridge over the Hamble.

His famous book *Rural Rides* gives an interesting picture of life in that district in the early nineteenth century. At that time, it was a predominantly turnip-growing district. Turnips must have been a staple crop, as Cobbett referred to them constantly, and judged a place largely by the quantity and quality of its turnips. Now the area is mainly given over to strawberry-growing. With modern methods of cultivation, the fruit can be produced for a great part of the year, and from about May until October, along all the main roads for miles around, wayside stalls are set up, with notices inviting motorists to stop and buy fresh strawberries. There is not quite the enjoyment in a bowl of strawberries and cream that there was when the season was so much shorter; nor is there quite the same pleasure in chrysanthemums, another industry of the district, when they can be had all the year round instead of just in the autumn. However, both fruit and flowers provide employment for a great many people, and so would probably have met with Cobbett's approval. He himself grew various exotic vegetables on his Botley farm.

He had violent prejudices against some people, places and things, including landlords, paper money, tea, London "The Wen", and shops, to which he preferred markets and fairs, and he railed against them unmercifully. If, however, any person, place, thing or activity pleased him, he could not say enough in its favour. One of his favourites, though a landlord, was a Mr Chamberlayne, who lived at Weston Grove, near Netley, and owned most of the land between that part of Southampton Water and the Hamble River. Cobbett was delighted with Mr Chamberlayne's estate and the way in which it was kept, the oak-trees, little hills and valleys and streams, and the views of Southampton Water, but above all he was delighted with Mr Chamberlayne himself. He was M.P. for Southampton, and a very talented and charming man, but his particular merit was that he paid his labourers 13/- a week, even when wages in other places went down to 8/- or even less. 13/- enabled labourers to live quite comfortably in those days, with enough to eat, and enough fuel, and they had good cottages and other perquisites when working for such a fair employer as Mr Chamberlayne. A Mrs Mears, of Durley, near Botley, earned Cobbett's favour by using a local grass called "dog's tail" to plait into straw for bonnets. She employed two girls at 6/- a week, considered by Cobbett a good wage for girls, and a milliner in Fareham bought the straw and made it up into bonnets and hats.

Between the Hamble River and Netley, on what was formerly the Chamberlayne estate, the Royal Victoria Military Hospital was built in 1856-63. This was a gigantic building, 1424 feet long, made in a somewhat Italianate style. It was not at all convenient, and Florence Nightingale disapproved of it, but it was still in use in the 1914-18 war, when wounded troops of many nationalities were sent there. Since 1966 it has been demolished, but the Royal Chapel belonging to it remains, and is an interesting Victorian building. The railway station is another Victorian period piece, rather in the style of Tite.

The Church of St Edward the Confessor, Netley, now also the parish church of Hound, a nearby hamlet, is by J. R. Sedding, 1886, and is a copy-book example of Victorian architecture. Under the tower is part of a thirteenth century tomb of a knight, formerly in the abbey. The Church of St Mary, Hound, not far away, is plain and attractive Early English, partly restored. It has a beautiful modern east window, by Patrick Reyntiens, 1959. The church plate was transferred to Netley. Netley and Weston are now built-up areas, but in Cobbett's time they were all part of the Chamberlayne estate, which included the beautiful ruins of Netley Abbey.

South Transept and Chapter House of Netley Abbey.

In 1239 the Bishop of Winchester, Peter des Roches, intended to found a Cistercian Monastery here, but his death prevented this, and King Henry III became the Founder and Patron of the Monastery, in March 1251. His name is carved on the base of one of the great pillars which formerly supported the central tower. Building then began in the beautiful style of the thirteenth century. For some three hundred years the monks lived in the seclusion of the monastery, according to the strict rule of the Cistercian Order. It has been said that the land which has no history is happy, and this might equally apply to Netley as well as to many other monasteries, But in 1536 came a rude shock, when the brethren learned that, although the monastery was a Royal Foundation, their house was to be dissolved. The abbot and monks were sent to the mother-house of Beaulieu on the opposite side of Southampton Water. All the fittings and furniture were burnt or otherwise destroyed, the bells were sounded for the last time and melted down, and the miserable skeleton of the abbey buildings handed over to the Commissioners of their Royal master, Henry VIII.

The site and buildings were granted by the King to William Paulet, who later became Marquis of Winchester. He converted the abbey buildings into a magnificent mansion. It is odd that, in spite of this conversion, very little indeed remains of this work of the Tudor period, whereas there is still a great deal of the medieval work. The Tudor conversion was carried out in red brick, which is still visible in some parts. This mansion continued to be occupied throughout the seventeenth century, but during the eighteenth century it fell upon evil days, the ruins being constantly pillaged for the sake of the excellent stone that was so readily available. A later owner was the Earl of Huntingdon, and he sold the ruins to a certain Walter Taylor, a builder, of Southampton. Being warned in a dream by an apparition dressed in monkish attire that he was about to die, he consulted a friend, who recommended him to have nothing to do with taking the stone from the abbey. His avarice, however, caused him to persist, and while he was superintending the taking down of the west front, a large stone fell upon him, causing immediate death. This happening was considered a Divine warning, and saved the ruins for the time being, but more destruction soon came from another quarter. The lady of Sir Nathaniel Howard, wishing to be in the front rank of the fashion of the day, bodily removed the north transept of the church and had it re-erected in Cranbury Park, Otterbourne, as a "cottage ornée".

During the eighteenth century many literary folk visited the ruins, and sang the praises of the beautiful foliage which, of course, was really sucking the life out of them. Thomas Gray, of "Elegy" fame, and Horace Walpole, were among these visitors, and it was Walpole who wrote the often-quoted, "They are not the ruins of Netley, but of Paradise: Oh, the purple Abbots, what a spot they had chosen to slumber in!" As time went on, however, slumber was not the objective of visitors to Netley. Hordes of trippers came to enjoy the beauty of the scene, and "fêtes champêtres" were the order of the day. Teas were obtainable from a cottage among the ruins, and were followed by music and dancing.

In the early nineteen-twenties, the ruins were handed over to the Ministry of Works (now Department of the Environment). The lovely wooded setting makes Netley one of the most beautiful of our abbeys. The repairs to the ruins were undertaken only just in time. Huge trees and bushes were cracking and destroying the stonework and tearing it apart, but all that has now been stopped, and enough is left to enable visitors to follow the Cistercian plan. The entrance to the building is in the south range. Here was the frater, but this has been entirely demolished. The gateway opens out into the cloister court, which was converted into a flower garden at the time of the Dissolution. Around it are the remains of the various offices of the abbey. On the opposite side of the cloister court is the church, which occupies the whole of the north side. It has suffered much more than any other part: the pillars and arcades have all been destroyed, but the outer walls remain throughout. In the east range is the chapter house: this was the meeting-place of the monks. It is entered from the cloister court by three arches. South of this is a long chamber, formerly vaulted, running north and south, which leads to the infirmary. Above this was the dorter and this led to the monastic rere-dorter which was flushed by a small stream. The west range is very ruinous. It formerly contained the buildings occupied by the lay brothers. A short distance to the north-east of the abbey is a small ruin of a medieval building. This is thought to have been the abbot's lodging.

On the opposite side of the road is Netley Castle, another of Henry VIII's chain of fortifications, built in 1542 and garrisoned until 1627. After that it became a residence. In the second half of the nineteenth century it was so much added to and altered, largely to the designs of the architect Sedding, that possibly all that can now be seen of the original fort is a Tudor archway in the main entrance. The Castle is now a convalescent home, and is not ordinarily open to the general public.

Netley Castle.

CHAPTER FOUR

Southampton

FROM 1836 until 1977, one could go on from Netley to Southampton by the "Floating Bridge" from Woolston. This was a ferry, carrying foot-passengers and vehicles. The inventor of Floating Bridges was James Rendell, a pupil of Telford. They were steam-powered, and the original one at Woolston was made of wood. The second one was made of iron. In the early days, they were used mainly by visitors to Netley Abbey, and one could obtain light refreshments on board. With the opening up of industry, particularly ship-building, in Woolston, the Floating Bridge became very useful to the workers. In the 1960s, steam power was replaced by diesel power, and three new ferries were built, but they became inadequate to the amount of traffic, and a great new toll bridge across the Itchen, just above the Floating Bridge, was opened in 1977 by Princess Alexandra. This bridge leads almost directly into the dock area, and the old town of Southampton.

The new (1977) bridge across the Itchen at Southampton.

The known history of Southampton begins about 70 A.D. with the building of a Roman fort, *Clausentum*, in a loop of the Itchen (near the present Northam Bridge) about 1½ miles from the centre of the modern town. The fort was defended by two deep ditches, and a massive wall across the landward side, but the site has been all built over and is now known as Bitterne Manor. However, the site has been fully excavated and many of the finds are to be seen in God's House Museum. Especially interesting are the coins of Carausius (287 A.D.) and Allectus (294 A.D.), already mentioned in connection with Portchester.

After the departure of the Romans, the Saxons formed a settlement further down the Itchen and on the opposite bank. This was *Hamwic*, and it occupied that particular part of the town which lies around St Mary's Church. There have been six St Mary's Churches on this site, and it is thought that the first one may have been founded about 634 A.D. by St Birinus, who brought back Christianity to the heathen Saxons. West of Hamwic was Hamtun. This part of Southampton suffered severely in the air raids of 1940. Before rebuilding began after the war, the opportunity was taken to excavate the whole area. The town seems to have been first called "Suthampton" in 962, the county having been "Hamtunscir" since 755.

Canute, the Danish king of England, was at one time in Southampton. The remains of a house in Porter's Lane, called the Long House, are sometimes known as Canute's Palace, but they cannot in fact be so, as he died in about 1035, and the house is not earlier than 1170. A public house, *The Canute*, is on the spot where, according to the legend, Canute sat and let the waves wash over him, as a rebuke to his courtiers, who foolishly flattered him by saying that he could control even the tides.

The Normans established a settlement at the promontory by the confluence of the rivers Itchen and Test. They defended this strong position by means of a turf wall, through which they built a stone gateway. This very typical Norman gateway still exists, but right inside the later Bargate. To this original gateway two drum towers were added during the thirteenth century, and a three-sided forebuilding, added during the fifteenth century, made it the most majestic town gateway in England, and worthy to rank with the famous "bars" of York. This was the principal entry into the old town, and distinguished visitors were always greeted here by the Mayor and Corporation. The south front of the Bargate has large Gothic windows dating from 1330, restored in 1865.

The Normans also built themselves a strong castle in the walled area, with a keep standing upon an artificial mound where it could command both the town and the ships coming up Southampton Water. This was a royal castle and the reigning monarch always lodged there (until Stuart times), when visiting the town. Not much of the castle remains, except the bailey wall, some

Southampton Bargate (from an old print, c.1810) seen from the north.

The south side of the Bargate.

good vaults, and the blocked castle water gate of a rather later date. Wealthy Norman merchants built themselves good stone houses, and there are remains of some of these, particularly the wrongly-named King John's House, near the Tudor House Museum. A magnificent and very typical example of a Norman chimney came to light as a result of the bombardment, and was moved to the Norman House, which is a great treasure because, though Norman castles and churches may be found all over England, good examples of Norman domestic architecture are distinctly rare. St Michael's Church has Norman crossing arches and a black marble Norman font. Several of the Norman vaults for storing wine and other goods remain in quite good condition, Quilter's Vault being one of the best. The King's Weigh-house, in which was the weigh-beam for weighing the wool, for some time one of the town's chief industries, was another Norman building, but unfortunately it was largely destroyed in the air raids.

At Portswood, at that time some way out of the town but now very well within it, St Denys Priory, of the Augustinian Order, was founded in 1125 by King Henry I, in memory of his son Prince William who was drowned in the wreck of the *White Ship*. Practically nothing remains of the Priory now, and, to a great number of people, St Denys now means the railway station.

The Normans built their town on the grid pattern, and the two most important streets were English Street and French Street, parallel to each other. At first the Saxon and Norman inhabitants kept themselves rather apart, but after a time, a common interest in trade drew them together and they settled down well enough. One of the prominent wealthy merchants of the twelfth century was Gervase le Riche. Among other good works, he took pity on the constant stream of pilgrims who landed at Southampton, probably after horrible crossings in very small and uncomfortable ships, on their way to visit the shrine of St Thomas à Becket at Canterbury. He built for them, and for some of the very poor people in the town, the "Maison Dieu" or "God's House". The pilgrims' lodgings and hospital were built round a quadrangle, and there was a chapel dedicated to St Julian, one of the patron saints of travellers. The Norman archway in the gateway remains, though most of the establishment was rebuilt in Victorian times. At one time it belonged to the Royal Family, and King Edward III presented it to Queen Philippa, who used some of its revenues to found Queen's College, Oxford, to which some Southampton boys can still win scholarships. The College remains owner of the almshouses.

St Mary's Church was largely rebuilt in Norman times, and was considered the Mother Church of Southampton. The Normans built several other churches, but only fragments of them remain.

Trade with the continent flourished in Norman times and for some time afterwards, though it had its fluctuations. Richard I and King John both granted charters to the town, and John visited it very frequently. In the time of his son, Henry III, the burgesses of Southampton purchased from Nicholas, Lord of the Manor of Shirley, the common, and magnificent tree-lined avenue, which form such a splendid entrance to Southampton from the north. Another event of the thirteenth century was the foundation of a Franciscan Friary, not far from God's House. The Friars looked after the poor and ill people of the town, and they also helped to give the town a good water-supply. Nicholas of Shirley presented them with a well of "sweet water" in the neighbourhood of Hill Lane, outside the walled town. They erected a conduit head over the spring, and a water house a little further in, and had the water brought in lead pipes to the town. This was possibly the first piped water supply in England, and the water was exported in great quantities for the use of English armies fighting abroad.

Parts of the Norman turf wall having been strengthened, or replaced, by stone ones, and some other defences, such as the early thirteenth century Arundel Tower at the north-west corner of the old town having been added, the inhabitants were lulled into a false sense of security, and a sudden French raid in 1338 caught them quite unprepared. It took place on a Sunday while they were at Mass. Nearly the whole town was burnt: looting and pillaging went on all day, and men, women and children were murdered indiscriminately. Eventually the invaders were somehow driven off, and, soon afterwards, west and south walls were added to the fortifications, thus making a complete circuit of wall, about 1¼ miles in length. More towers were added at strategic positions, including the Polymond Tower on the north-east corner, and the curiously-named Catchcold Tower a little south of the Arundel Tower. These three still exist, and there were several more, no longer standing, near the south-west corner. As some of the merchants' stone-built houses opened straight on to the beach of the River Test, the sentry's walk was built out on a series of arches known as the Arcade. Some of these houses were Norman, and it is possible to see where the windows and doors have been blocked up in order to incorporate the houses into the scheme of defence, a probably unique feature. Two gun-ports of fourteenth century date have been driven through the blocking walls. They can easily be distinguished, as they take the form of vertical slits, having rounded openings at the bottom. The walls were completed by the fourteenth century, some 30 feet high, and containing 29 towers and 7 gateways, of which four still exist.

The Arcade, on the western section of Southampton's city walls.

The Westgate, just south of the Arcade, though not very distinguished architecturally, is rich in history. Through it marched the troops, under Edward III and his son Edward the Black Prince, when they were embarking for the French campaign which resulted in the great victory of Crecy in 1346. Nearly sixty years later, more troops led by Henry V, marched through the Westgate on the way to the famous victory of Agincourt, 1415. Just before they were due to start, a conspiracy to murder the King was discovered. The plotters were three noblemen, Richard Plantagenet, Earl of Cambridge, Henry, Lord Scrope, and Sir Thomas Grey. They were discovered just in time to save the king's life, and quickly tried and executed. One or two historians place these sinister events at Portchester, but it is generally believed that they took place at Southampton.

Next to the Westgate is a timbered building known as the "Guard Room", but now thought to have been a Tudor merchant's store.

The town had suffered from a severe visitation of the Black Death in 1348, with the dead lying about unburied in the streets. There had also been intermittent fighting with the French, since the beginning of the Hundred Years' War in 1337, and another attack by the French on the town in 1377, fortunately unsuccessful, and there had been a long period of depression, but by the time of Henry V, prosperity seems to have returned. Between the times when troops were marching out of the Westgate to attack France, there was considerable trade between the two countries, and the beautiful old Wool-house, still standing in Bugle Street, dates from about this time. It has a magnificent chestnut roof, and some buttresses of a rather later date. God's House Tower, at the south-east corner of the old walled city, was the latest fortification, and was completed a little before the time of the Battle of Agincourt. It is a "spur work", jutting out so that it could command both the Itchen and the Test. It also controlled the sluice gate, which kept the moat at the correct level.

Southampton Westgate, seen from the east. To the left is the so-called Guard Room, more probably a Tudor merchant's store, and beyond can be seen the modern Post House Hotel and the cranes of the New Docks.

The Wool-house, with the former Victorian Yacht Club, now University Air Squadron, and the modern Post House Hotel in the background.

God's House Tower.

Henry V made some more successful expeditions to France, but in 1422, at the height of his success and popularity, he died suddenly of a fever, leaving his baby son, only nine months old, to succeed him as Henry VI and reign from 1422 until 1461. His reign was not at all happy, being marred by the Wars of the Roses, which broke out in 1455 and lasted until long after his death. Before this, however, he had married, in 1445, Margaret of Anjou, a girl of only fifteen. They were first married by proxy in France, and she then proceeded to Southampton, and after a terrible Channel crossing lasting a week, she was allowed four days' rest with the nuns of the Maison Dieu, before meeting her husband, whom she had never seen, at the Castle.

This was one of the prosperous times in the town. In this same year, the town was sufficiently important to warrant the granting of "Incorporation for every of one Mayor, 2 Bailiffs and Burgesses". There had been mayors and charters before, but this charter put things on a firm basis. Two years later the town was granted another charter, whereby it had its own Sheriff as distinct from the Sheriff of Hampshire. The Mayor became "Admiral of the Port", his jurisdiction extending from Hurst and Lymington on the west to Langstone and Portsmouth on the east. In 1451 Henry VI confirmed all former grants, including the Mayor's title. The "Admiral of the Port" had very wide powers. He could claim all wrecks and had jurisdiction over the fisheries, and on a map of that date are shown two gallows, each with its victim! Even today the Mayor still holds the courtesy title, although his duties as Admiral of the Port actually ceased in Victorian times. A silver oar is still carried before him on ceremonial occasions, as a symbol of his authority.

Southampton was something of a naval port during the reigns of Henry V and Henry VI, though it afterwards reverted much more to merchant shipping. Henry VI was not a warrior as his father had been, and during his reign England lost all her French possessions except Calais. His unhappy life was finally brought to an end by his murder in the Tower of London in 1471.

Southampton continued to do good trade in spite of the Wars of the Roses, and after Henry VII came to the throne in 1485, he did much to promote it further. The Reformation saw the closure of both St Denys Priory and the Friary, but the town still prospered. Leland, Chronicler and Antiquary to Henry VIII visited Southampton about 1540, and reported to the king that "the glory of the Castle is its Keep, which is both large and fair". He also noted that the High Street (formerly English Street) was "one of the fairest in all England for timber building". The beautiful Tudor House, still standing and now a museum, was built at about this time for Sir Richard Lyster, Chief Baron of the King's Exchequer. Henry VIII and Edward VI both visited Southampton, but the town became rather less prosperous during their reigns.

Tudor House.

After the death of Edward VI, when his half-sister Mary was Queen, King Philip of Spain landed at Southampton on his way to marry Mary at Winchester. This marriage was not at all popular. Philip stayed three nights at Southampton and attended mass at the Chapel of the Holy Rood. He left the town by the Bargate, with an escort of about 3,000 men, some English, some Spanish, in drenching rain, damping what should have been a happy occasion.

The country in general was relieved when Mary died in 1558 and Elizabeth I came to the throne. When the threat of Spanish invasion became urgent, every port of any importance was asked to provide two ships and enough men to man them, but Southampton at that time was not able to provide them. Fortunately, owing to the defeat of the Armada, the invasion never took place. In September 1591, Queen Elizabeth visited Southampton with all her court and stayed four days, during which she was most lavishly entertained, at the then very large sum of £98, part of which was spent on re-gilding the Civic mace.

When Elizabeth died in 1603, and James VI of Scotland became James I of England, it was hoped that he would be tolerant in church affairs. A petition was signed by about 825 Puritans, but James proved to be very intolerant, and said of the petitioners that he would "make them conform or harry them out of the land". As the situation grew worse, a company of people agreed to emigrate. They purchased a small ship, the *Speedwell* of 60 tons, a vessel no larger than a modern excursion steamer, and hired the *Mayflower*, of 180 tons. Both ships lay alongside the West Quay while preparations were being made for departure. On 15th August 1620, the two ships were ready for the voyage to the New World. Unfortunately the *Speedwell* sprang a leak, and it was decided that she could not be used, so both ships put in at Plymouth, and all the passengers and crew were transferred to the *Mayflower*, where conditions must have been very cramped indeed. After a very rough voyage of 67 days, land was sighted and was named "New Plymouth". A memorial to these brave adventurers, "The Pilgrim Fathers", was erected in 1913, just outside the Westgate, the quay from which the voyage started. The memorial consists of a slim tower with a cupola, and a model of the *Mayflower* on the top, and stands in what is now the Mayflower Park, where many events such as the annual Boat Show are held.

By this time the Norman Castle had been allowed to fall into disrepair, and was no longer considered suitable for the entertainment of royalty, so James I sold it for £2,075. 0. 1¼. One wonders what items were included for the final 1¼d.

Southampton did not play much part in the great Civil War, although Winchester and Romsey, both within a dozen miles, saw much fighting.

In the reign of Charles II came the tragedy of the Great Plague. It was carried to Southampton by a child, who had been sent from London in the hope of avoiding it. The outbreak was aggravated by an unusually hot summer. Some old women were paid a few shillings a week to look after the plague victims: presumably they must either have had the plague already and recovered from it, or have been so poor that they were ready to earn money even in this dangerous way. Charles II deeply sympathised with the stricken town and sent a sum of £50 and a surgeon at his own expense. Eventually the plague died down, and in 1669 Southampton was honoured by a Royal visit. The townspeople, led by the Mayor, welcomed the king outside the Bargate, and presented him with a purse containing 150 guineas. Pepys, that inimitable diarist, described the scene. He noted that the High Street was "one most gallant street", and that the town walls were still standing and still encircled the town.

Celia Fiennes, who rode all over England on horseback, visited Southampton towards the end of the seventeenth century, and described it as a "very clean neat town and the streets well pitched and kept so by their carrying all their carriages on sleds as they do in Holland, and permit no cart to go about in the town and keep it clean swept" . . . She added, however, that the town was "almost forsooke and neglected" and that the trade had failed, "tho' by most its thought the best scittuated port for ships to ride and take their provision in, and so capeable of trading". She described the castle as being in ruins and the fortifications neglected.

In 1685 a charter was granted to "the Governors and Corporation of white-paper makers". Three of the original members were connected with the French Protestant Church. One of the family, Henri Portal, had escaped from France concealed in a barrel. He learned all about the printing trade and did so well that he was able to set up for himself at Woodmill, a northern suburb of Southampton. He finally obtained the monopoly for making the special paper upon which our banknotes are printed, and the firm still holds this monopoly.

During the eighteenth century, after a long period of depression, the fortunes of the town began to improve, and in 1750 an event occurred which changed the whole fortune and character of the town. Frederick, then Prince of Wales, while staying in the New Forest, was persuaded to bathe at Southampton for the benefit of his health. He enjoyed it, concluded that the sea water was "both salubrious and invigorating", and returned several times. Where the Prince led, Society followed. A chalybeate spring was also discovered, the water of which, impregnated with iron salts, was said to "open all manner of obstructions" and to be "of astonishing service in tedious and obstinate agues, black and yellow jaundice as well as the scurvy, green sickness and even paralytic disorders". The Prince may not have suffered from any of these complaints, but at least he felt definitely better for his bathes from the Western Shore (where the new docks are now situated) and the town, which had been a gradually dying port, became an exceedingly prosperous health resort "patronised by the nobility and gentry". So Prince Frederick did for Southampton what George III did later for Weymouth, and George IV did for Brighton.

The townsfolk were very quick to exploit the budding resort; hotels and lodging-houses sprang up like mushrooms, and an enterprising business-man named Martin erected, in 1761, the Long Rooms, which were "fitted up at great expense in a most elegant manner". They became the resort of all the rank and fashion, and the centre of much gossip and scandal. During the summer season, which stretched from May until October, balls were held there twice a week. A regular standard of behaviour was insisted on, and a code of manners was drawn up and strictly followed. Gentleman had to leave their swords at the door, and were not allowed to dance in boots. Balls were to "begin as soon as possible after 7 p.m. and finish at 11, even in the middle of a dance" and there were many other rules which read oddly today. Adjacent to the Long Rooms were the Baths, also erected by Martin near the Westgate. In these baths, it was stated, "Ladies and Gentlemen can bathe at any time and in any depth of water by means of the artificial bottoms of the baths which are raised or let down at pleasure by means of winches". There was also an Observation Chamber for people who liked to watch "the evolutions of the bathers in the water", a popular entertainment. The rough ground outside the Bargate was tidied up, and winding paths were constructed, giving glimpses of the sparkling sea water below. The chalybeate spring was also in this part of the town, and was directed into a basin on a fluted pedestal: this has been preserved in the Tudor House Museum.

Many celebrities came to the newly-established resort, including King George III and his brother the Duke of Gloucester with their wives and families, Horace Walpole, who wrote that the town was crowded, and the poet Cowper, who thought that the view across the Test towards the New Forest was one of the most beautiful that he had ever seen. (Would he think so now?)

Edward Gibbon, author of *The Decline and Fall of the Roman Empire* spent a few months in Southampton in 1762 as a Captain in the Hampshire Militia. He was made a Freeman of the town. He gave a dinner to the Mayor, the Corporation and his fellow officers, and spent altogether £13. He records that the bill would have been larger, had not one of the Aldermen provided the turtle for the soup!

Another patron of the spa was the second Marquess of Lansdowne, who purchased the site of the old castle and demolished the remains of the Norman keep. On its mound he erected a house in the Gothic style of Horace Walpole's Strawberry Hill house. (A style of architecture known as "Strawberry Hill Gothic" to distinguish it from genuine old Gothic). Unfortunately this only lasted fourteen years and was demolished in its turn, a sad architectural loss. The Marquess played an active part in the life of the town, and it was he who presented the statue of George III dressed as a Roman Emperor on the south side of the Bargate. The Marchioness used to drive about the town in a light carriage drawn by eight little New Forest ponies, much to the amusement of Jane Austen, who lived with her mother in Castle Square from 1806 to 1809. She much enjoyed the gaiety of Southampton Spa, which was considered by many people as nothing short of an earthly paradise. There were picnics in the country, which still came up to the town walls, trips by boat to Netley Abbey, card parties, dances, and sometimes balls at the *Dophin Hotel*, in the magnificent Assembly Room, now the Coffee Room. The *Dolphin*, and another Georgian Hotel, the *Star*, very fortunately survived when almost the whole of the High Street was destroyed by bombs in 1940. The bow-windows of the *Dolphin*, said to be the largest in England, look out on to High Street. The *Star* still has a pillar in its doorway advertising "Coach to London, Sundays excepted, Alresford and Alton. Performs 10 hours". There were many fast coaches to Winchester and London, but transport within the town was mainly by sedan chair, of which one is preserved in the Tudor House Museum.

With the popularity of the spa, the town spread out beyond its old walls, and many elegant villas and other houses were erected. Some still remain, in Carlton Crescent, Rockstone Place and other parts of the town. A stairway, known as the Forty Steps, was built from what is now Western Esplanade up the old walls to Albion Place, near Catchcold Tower.

The spa began to decline in the first half of the nineteenth century, as the possibilities of Southampton as a great port came to be realised, and in course of time the Long Rooms and other spa buildings were demolished, and the town's prosperity was gained in other ways. An Act of Parliament was passed to allow the start of work on docks, warehouses and piers and a Board of Harbour Commissioners was appointed. A great deal of land was reclaimed from the sea, including the part where Prince Frederick and his friends had bathed, and gradually, over the years, the magnificent docks that may be seen today were built up, making Southampton one of the foremost ports of the world. The Royal Pier was built in 1833, and by 1842 the Peninsular and Oriental Steam Navigation Company, and the Royal Mail Steam Packet Company were both running regular services to far parts of the world, and other famous shipping lines followed suit.

The fine docks, with six miles of quays, are divided into two sections. The Eastern Docks include the Ocean Terminal, the Queen Elizabeth II Terminal, opened by the Queen herself in 1966, and the Princess Alexandra Dock used largely by the cross-channel car ferries. Southampton has been a seaport from early times; it was the coming of the railways to connect it with London and the double high water every tide that brought it to the forefront in the second half of the nineteenth century. Its success was assured when Royal Mail, Union Castle and Cunard steamship lines selected it as their main British port. Once a famous passenger port with dry docks, ship building and repairing facilities and, later a refrigeration dock, it is today one of the leading container ports handling large quantities of cargo. Tours of the docks are sometimes arranged by boat or bus from the Civic Centre. It is sad to think that of all the beautiful liners which used the docks, including the "Queens", practically none are now left on regular service and only a few survive for cruises.

The railroad was growing up at the same time as the docks and steamships. The London and Southampton Railway was partly opened in 1839. In the meantime the line was opened from London to Basingstoke: then came a gap of about 15 miles which travellers had to cross by coach, followed by another rail journey from Winchester to Southampton. Presumably the people of Southampton were so thrilled with the prospect of quicker travel, that they were prepared to put up with two changes. In 1840, however, the gap was closed. The Southampton terminus of the line was a handsome, Italianate station, designed by Sir William Tite, a famous early Victorian architect. Very fortunately, this was another building which escaped damage during the bombing of 1940.

In 1878, a line of horse-drawn tramcars was laid down, to serve the needs of people who lived in the houses outside the old town but had their businesses still in the central part. The trams were each drawn by two horses, and their routes were gradually extended to all parts of the borough. The cars had open tops. In 1900 came the electric car, and a problem was how to allow the trams with their trolley-poles to pass under the Bargate. The iconoclasts wanted to make this an excuse to demolish the Bargate as an anachronism, and a lively battle took place in the columns of the local press. Very fortunately, the preservationists won, and the problem was solved by lowering the road, but the game of "shooting the Bargate" was a dangerous one until the tops of the cars were closed in.

Southampton continued, throughout its history, to be an embarkation point for troops in war-time, thousands passing through it in the Boer War,

A Southampton horse-drawn tramcar.   (*Photograph by courtesy of Southern Evening Echo, Southampton*)

more in the 1948-18 war, and millions in the 1939-45 war. The loss of the huge White Star liner *Titanic*, which struck an iceberg and sank on her maiden voyage, was a terrible shock to the town, as she was manned largely by Southampton men. There is a memorial to her on the Common, north of the Bargate. This tragedy was followed by the sinking of the Cunarder *Lusitania*, as an act of war in 1915. The shock and horror of this event contributed to bringing the United States into the war. No bombs fell on Southampton during that war, but in the Second World War the town suffered terribly when, in 1940, nearly all the buildings in Above Bar Street and High Street were flattened by high explosives, and there were very heavy casualties. King George VI came down to Southampton and walked down the principal streets, piled high with debris, and did a great deal to cheer people up.

Of the medieval churches, St Mary's and All Saints were almost entirely destroyed, and Holy Rood was too seriously damaged to be used as a church any more. What remains of it has been made into a memorial to merchant seamen, and its beautiful lectern, which luckily survived, has been moved to St Michael's, the only church in the old town to remain intact. St Mary's has been rebuilt. The Civic Centre, built only in 1933, on West Marlands, was also partly destroyed, but has been restored. It has a tall tower containing nine bells, upon which a carillon plays the tune of "O God, our Help in Ages Past". This popular hymn was composed by Isaac Watts, a native of Southampton, to whom there is a statue near the Civic Centre. The citizens are thus constantly reminded of one of our best-known hymn-writers.

Southampton became a City in 1964, and no doubt the rebuilt city will carry on the traditions of magnificent courage, learned the hard way during many centuries.

Henry Robinson Hartley left £100,000 for educational purposes and the Hartley Institution was open by Lord Palmerston in 1862. It was incorporated as the Hartley University College in 1902, and received its Royal Charter as University of Southampton in 1952. At that time it had under 1,000 students but the number has increased rapidly and is expected to reach 7,000 in the early 1980s. The architect of many of the modern buildings, including the Nuffield Theatre, was Sir Basil Spence.

"The Saints", Southampton's famous football team, is usually well up in League Football. In 1976 they became only the sixth Second Division team to win the Football Association Challenge Cup when they beat Manchester United by one goal to nil at Wembley. Southampton is also the Headquarters of the Hampshire County Cricket Club, and there are yacht clubs and every kind of sport and recreation.

Broadcasting is represented in Southampton by the B.B.C.'s Radio Solent and the I.T.V. Southern Television. These and local newspapers provide news of past and forthcoming events in the Solent area.

CHAPTER FIVE

West Shore of Southampton Water

M ILLBROOK, Redbridge and Totton form the north-west part of
Southampton, where the River Test widens out and flows into
Southampton Water. Totton is a mainly modern, built-up area, beginning
where the road and railway cross the Test. South of Totton, and joined on to
it, is Eling, a small port from old times. A mill there was mentioned in the
Domesday Survey. The old village of Eling is approached from Totton by what
was a tollbridge, so that it has not been too much spoiled by traffic. The
church, St Mary, is also the parish church of Totton. It is the oldest church in
the New Forest area, and it is thought that a chapel was founded there as long
ago as A.D.850. There is still some Saxon work in the church, including arches
in the north and south aisles and parts of some small windows. There were
repairs and additions in Norman times, and some of the Norman work can still
be seen. Eling had connections with the Abbey of Jumiéges in Normandy, and
in the thirteenth and fourteenth centuries the church was enlarged in the
style of the abbey. The bases of the pillars are all of different designs, as at
Jumiéges and other churches in Normandy, though the general style of Eling
Church is Early English. The tower is fifteenth century. Behind the altar is a
"Last Supper" believed to have been painted by Marziale, a pupil of
Leonardo, in the early sixteenth century: the picture includes the dogs eating
the crumbs. It may possibly have been commissioned by Lord Sandys, then
patron of the church, for this very place. There are some Rysbrack monuments
and many other interesting features, and the church also possesses a wonderful
set of records dating from 1537.

The Grange and the Old Rectory are two pleasant old houses. There is
also an old tide-mill, of which definite records exist from 1418, when it was
leased out by Winchester College. The mill was working until comparatively
recently, and could grind about 3 tons of grain on a good tide. The Eling
Sailing Club used part of the mill as a club-room for a time. Winchester
College eventually handed over the mill to the New Forest District Council,
and there is a hope that, with the aid of the Solent Protection Society and
similar bodies, the mill and the little harbour will always be preserved. Isaac
Watts, the well-known early eighteenth century hymn-writer, is said to have
written, "There is a land of pure delight" in Eling churchyard, inspired by the
view across Southampton Water, but his "Sweet fields beyond the swelling

floods, Are dressed in living green" is now far from the truth, the fields being entirely covered by houses, tower blocks of flats, and industries, with scarcely a green blade to be seen.

Yachts anchored by Eling tide mill.

South-east of Eling is the great Marchwood Power Station, considered quite a fine example of British industrial architecture, though it might have astonished Cobbett. He only approved of machinery if it could be proved to cause no unemployment. He had been against the Luddite anti-machinery riots, but later had come to have more sympathy with the rioters, and he would probably have regarded Marchwood with considerable suspicion. The village of Marchwood lies a mile or so inland and is still comparatively rural, and from there one has only to cross the A326 road to be on the edge of the New Forest.

The next village is Dibden, which still has some fields and woods. The parish church, All Saints, was the first to be destroyed by an air-raid in the 1939-45 war. It was hit by incendiary bombs, in June 1940, and only the walls and an empty tower were left standing. The bells fell on to the font, and broke it into eleven pieces. After the war, however, the church was splendidly restored, and re-consecrated in 1955. The early Norman font was put together again, and some remains of the bells melted down to make two new ones. The chancel and chancel arch are thirteenth century, and there is a beautiful modern east window, by Derek Wilson, of the risen and triumphant Christ.

It is thought that the family of Charles Dibdin came originally from Dibden village, though he was born in Southampton in 1745, the youngest of a family of eighteen. He was an actor, author, and composer of operettas as well as of his famous sea-songs, of which he wrote well over 1,000. These were considered so inspiring and encouraging to British sailors, in the wars against France, that the government in 1803 awared him a pension of £200 a year. His best-known song, "Tom Bowling" was written in memory of his eldest brother, Captain Thomas Dibdin, who died on a voyage home from India.

Hythe, formerly a village on the west bank of Southampton Water, is now a small town, partly built for people working at Fawley, and extending inland to the verge of the New Forest at Dibden Purlieu. It still has some pleasant old streets near the shore, and very good views across Southampton Water to Southampton to the north and Netley to the east. There is a pier, 700 yards long, built in 1879, from which a ferry runs to Southampton. An electric railway runs along the pier. Hythe church, St John's, is of Victorian brick with stone dressings, by John Scott, 1874. Forest Lodge, a large house, partly eighteenth and partly nineteenth century, between Hythe and Fawley, had romantic landscaped grounds, of which some features remain.

From Forest Lodge, almost down to Calshot right on the Solent, now extends the vast Esso Oil Refinery at Fawley. This was started on a small scale in 1920, but was enormously increased after the Second World War, and now covers well over 1,000 acres. This is the most striking industrial landscape in the Solent area or, possibly, in the British Isles. Seen from the air, the rows of oil storage tanks have rather the appearance of a giant's draught-board. From the ground level the vast array of factory chimneys is more noticeable, these having been made 450 feet high so that the fumes would not be objectionable in the surrounding countryside. The "everlasting flame" from one of the chimneys can be seen at nights from all the higher parts of Hampshire. The oil-tankers, now the world's biggest ships, come from the Middle East to their

The electric railway along Hythe Pier.

jetties at Fawley, and can take advantage of the unusual double high tides.

As far as can be ascertained there are at least two possible explanations for this phenomena. One is that the first high tide comes up the Solent and is followed by the second up Spithead two hours later. The other suggests that the incoming tide along the English Channel gives Southampton its first normal high tide which is followed two hours later by the back wash northwards of the tide from the Cherbourg peninsula on the French coast opposite giving the

Fawley Refinery looking rather surrealist in the early morning mist.

second high water, two hours later than the first.

Other, related industries such as chemicals and butyl rubber, have been added to the original refineries, and over 2,000 people are employed. Good industrial relations have always been a feature here. A pleasant little rural touch is provided by a shepherd and his dog, and a flock of sheep whose job it is to eat down any grass amid the industrial complex, and so to lessen any fire risk.

Fawley Refinery from the east shore of Southampton Water.

On the site there formerly stood Cadland House and grounds, designed by Capability Brown. Unfortunately, this was demolished, but trees and shrubs have been planted all along the landward side of the refinery, both to improve the looks and to deaden some of the sounds. Half a mile away, on Ashlett Creek, there are a tide-mill and granary, 1818, now used as an Esso Recreational Club. Fawley was at one time noted for its cherries, and it had "a merrie Fair at which cherries were picked and eaten", the pickers frequently becoming almost too "merrie".

Fawley church, All Saints, like Dibden church, was a victim of enemy action, but was not quite so seriously damaged. The chancel was largely destroyed, and the north and south chapels injured, but the church was still able to be used, and after the war it was very well restored, and re-dedicated in 1954. It retains a Norman arch over the west door, and a Norman capital on the south-west pillar of the tower and a Norman window in the choir. Under the chancel window outside, there is one small window believed to be Saxon, perhaps formerly a leper squint. The nave arches are thirteenth century, and the tracery of the chancel window is transition between Early English and Decorated. There are several memorials to the Drummond family, of Cadland, who were considerable benefactors to the church. In the south chapel there is a

Calshot Castle. Henry VIII's drum tower is dwarfed by the modern radar tower and the vast Fawley power station, the chimney of which can be seen from all over the Solent.

model Tristan fishing boat, given by natives of Tristan da Cunha who took refuge at Calshot after the volcano eruption in 1961, and attended services in Fawley church. A little further south, at Ower, is the Fawley Power Station, even bigger than the Marchwood one, though built partly underground. Its chimney dwarfs even those of the refinery.

The last place on the west shore of Southampton Water, where it opens out into the Solent proper, is Calshot. Calshot Spit is a narrow isthmus running from south to north up Southampton Water. At the south end of the spit is a holiday area with beach huts, and at the north end is Calshot Castle, another of Henry VIII's forts, built of stone from Netley and Beaulieu Abbeys. It was small, but very strong, and had a garrison of only twenty. It has a low, round tower with a parapet, and is in a fair state of preservation, but is not being put to any use at the time of writing. With Calshot Castle on the west shore, and Netley Castle on the east, Southampton Water must have been well defended in Tudor and Stuart times.

From 1913 until 1961, Calshot was used as a flying base. The Royal Naval Air Service was formed in October, 1912, and soon afterwards the Admiralty set up Naval Air Stations to defend the British coast, from Scapa Flow round to Pembroke Dock. Calshot Naval Air Station was opened in March, 1913. At that time some of the personnel were stationed in the castle, and others round about, and the first Commanding Officer flew over every day from Southsea in his own seaplane. During the 1914-18 war the Station was very active in training air crews and in helping with coastal and channel defence. One officer who trained at Calshot was E. R. Moon, one of the pioneers of flying, who had flown his own monoplane as early as 1910 and who, after an adventurous career, was killed in a flying boat crash in 1920.

Some of the Calshot personnel were in camp at Eaglehurst, a mile or two to the south, and in 1917 a little railway was set up between Eaglehurst and Calshot. This lasted until 1948, and one of its two engines was later sent to the Talyllyn Railway in Wales, where it is still running. All sorts of flying-boats and seaplanes were used, many of them built at Gosport. Between the wars Calshot was also a centre for boat-building, marine engine fitting and motor-boat crew training for the Royal Air Force. Lawrence of Arabia (Aircraftman Shaw) was there several times during his R.A.F. years.

The R.A.F. High Speed Flight, which was formed at Felixstowe in Suffolk, moved to Calshot in July 1927 to complete its preparations for the Schneider Trophy race to be held in Venice later that year and to be near the aircraft maker's works at Woolston near Southampton. Flight Lieutenant Webster in a Supermarine 5, N220, won the event in Venice at 281.65 m.p.h. with Flight Lieutenant Worsley in another Supermarine second at 273 m.p.h. In 1929 the High Speed Flight again moved from Felixstowe to Calshot for the race off Ryde, Isle of Wight which was won by Flying Officer Waghorn at

328.63 m.p.h. in a Supermarine S.6A, N247. A few days later Flight Lieutenant Stainforth set a new World Speed Record of 336.31 m.p.h. only to have it broken by Squadron Leader Orlebar with a speed of 355.8 m.p.h. Thus the Flight set two World Records and won the trophy for the second consecutive time. In 1931 the team again left Felixstowe for Calshot and won outright for Britain the Schneider Trophy when Flight Lieutenant Boothman in a Supermarine S.6B, S1595, won at 340.8 m.p.h. Later Stainforth in an S.6B, S1596, set a world speed record of 379.05 m.p.h. which, on 29th September in S6B, S1595, he broke again with a speed of 407.5 m.p.h.

In the Second World War, Calshot was used for training crews for Coastal Command aircraft and for air-sea rescues, and for the maintenance and repair of flying boats and other marine craft. Several craft from Calshot took part in the Dunkirk rescue operation, and some were lost. Sunderland flying-boats were used after the war to take part in the Berlin Air Lift.

Calshot continued to be used for maintenance work until 1961, when it closed as a Service Establishment. It had done an enormous amount of very useful work, but had not been the ideal place for flying-boats and seaplanes, because of the difficulties of taking off in the rather overcrowded waters of Southampton Water and the Solent. Of recent years, Calshot has been the scene of an exciting venture by the Hampshire Education Authority, the Calshot Activities Centre. Young people aged from thirteen upwards can take courses, under expert instruction, in adventurous activities such as sailing, canoeing, navigation, sea-angling, field work of various kinds, bird-watching, archery and team games. Some of the old R.A.F. buildings have been adapted for these purposes, and even rock-climbing and skiing can be learnt there. There are two residential hostels, Lawrence House, called after Lawrence of Arabia, and Houston House, called after Lady Houston, who helped greatly in financing the Schneider Trophy teams. With the Solent to the east and south, and the New Forest nearby to the west, Calshot is ideally placed for all these stimulating activities.

Eaglehurst is in the woods, and can only be seen from the sea. Most of the ferries and other shipping pass close to the Calshot Spit Lightship, and from here there is a good view of Eaglehurst tower and house. Luttrell's Tower, built by Temple Simon Luttrell in the eighteen century, is of the Gothic type. From its cellar it has a passage to the beach, believed to have been used by smugglers. The tower was also used by Marconi, who sent early wireless messages from it to his yacht *Electra*. There is a small classical temple in the grounds, but the estate is not open to the public, being now owned by the Landmark Trust, which preserves interesting houses and lets them to suitable tenants.

From Eaglehurst, the Solent shore runs south-westward, with pretty woodlands coming almost down to the water's edge. From Stanmore Point, the shore runs due west to Lepe. This is a charming little place, with a row of old coastguard cottages and a few other buildings, and a shingle beach with a stream, the Darkwater, running out across it, and beautiful views across to the Isle of Wight. It is said that, in the past, there was a causeway by which one could cross to the Island at low tide, and in the middle was a narrow channel over which men and horses could "leap": hence the name. This is doubted by historians, but even now, the water is so far out at low tide, that it is possible to imagine the truth of the story.

It is known that Lepe was quite an important landing and embarkation point. It may possibly have been a port in Roman times, and there may have been a Roman road from Lepe to Dibden, but historians differ on this. The Black Prince is believed to have embarked some of his troops for France from Lepe, and other Royalty occasionally landed there or embarked from there, including the unfortunate Charles I when he was taken to the Isle of Wight. Lepe was certainly quite a well-known port in medieval times, and in the eighteenth century three men-of-war were built there, the largest being H.M.S. *Europe*, of 64 guns. In modern times, Lepe and all this part of the Solent was a tremendous hive of activity for the D.Day operations.

Lepe Country Park, run by the Countryside Committee of the Hampshire County Council, consists of about 120 acres of land between Lepe and Calshot, where the public can picnic, swim, fish and walk in delightful surroundings. There is a good car park and other facilities, not too obtrusive, on the site of an old gun-emplacement. Bathing is not possible at low tide, as, when the sea is right out, the shore consists largely of mud, in which it is possible to stick, and then to be overwhelmed when the tide comes in again. This has happened occasionally, and people have been rescued with difficulty. At high tide, there are sometimes rather dangerous currents, so visitors who want to swim would do well to consult people with local knowledge before going in. When the summer season is over, Lepe is a very quiet little place, and may be much enjoyed by the less sociable visitors.

CHAPTER SIX

Beaulieu River

NEAR Lepe, and at Stone Point just east of it, there are beacons to mark where yachts may safely enter the Beaulieu River. Needs Oar (Ore on some maps) Point is opposite Lepe on the west bank of the river, about a mile away, and the Beaulieu Spit, sometimes covered with water, runs eastward from Needs Oar. There are bird sanctuaries on both sides of the river between Lepe and Needs Oar, where the land is marshy, and rare birds seen there have included the osprey. At Needs Oar Point is the club house of the Beaulieu River Sailing Club. The Beaulieu River is one of the prettiest and most popular yachting centres of the Solent, and yachts can enter at almost any time except very low tide. Much of the river runs through delightful woodland scenery, and is within what is called the "perambulation" of the New Forest.

The mouth of the Beaulieu River.

The rights over the river belong to the owner (at present the third Baron Montagu of Beaulieu) and trustees of the Beaulieu Estate. These rights were granted by King John to the monks of Beaulieu, and have belonged to the owners of Beaulieu ever since. This means that yachtsmen pay for landing, moorage, boomage and other nautical charges, though these are not very high. The owner of Beaulieu also owns the bed of the river, the flotsam and jetsam, the fishing, and sundry other rights. The river is well looked after by the trustees and a harbour master. As in the Hamble River, visiting yachtsmen need to make sure in advance that they can have a mooring, as the river is extremely popular.

At Needs Oar the channel of the river turns north-west and after about another half-mile, at Gin's Farm, turns almost due north. Near Gin's Farm, on the west bank, there is a quay, and nearby is the headquarters and club house of the Royal Southampton Yacht Club. Gin's, sometimes spelt Ginnes, Gynnes or even Genes, is a charming old farm-house dating well back into history. In Tudor and Stuart times it was occupied by a family named Kemp or Kempe. In 1580 a Thomas Kemp married Mary Oglander, of the very well-known family of Nunwell, in the Isle of Wight. There is a deed showing that another Kemp leased Gin's Farm from 1616 to 1669 at £16 a year. In 1809 there is a record that a stranger, probably a ship-wrecked sailor, was washed up on the shore there. Later, the farm was occupied by the Brown family. At one time there were salterns, and some old cottages connected with them, a little further north. The industry was important in the eighteenth century, and there was a Salt Officer at Beaulieu, but nothing remains of it now.

Opposite Gin's, on the east bank, is Exbury Point, where there are private moorings, and at Gilbury Hard, a little further up the east bank, there is a public landing place, from which a footpath runs to Exbury (also approachable by road from Lepe or Beaulieu). Exbury House, built 1964-5 by the Rothschilds on the site of the kitchen garden of a former house, has a garden open to the public at times well advertised in local papers: it is particularly beautiful in the bluebell and azalea season. Exbury church, 1907, in good Victorian Gothic style, has a Purbeck marble font, c. 1300, brought from an old church at Lower Exbury.

Between Gin's Farm and Buckler's Hard, on the west bank, Henry, first Baron Montagu, started some oyster beds in the 1880s. They were not successful, but in the 1939-45 war, parts of the Mulberry Harbour used in the Normandy landings were built on this very spot.

Almost opposite Gilbury Hard, where the channel of the river again turns west, is the famous Buckler's Hard. This is a hamlet consisting of one wide street, sloping down to the river, of eighteenth century houses, planned by John, Duke of Montagu in 1724. He intended to make Buckler's Hard a large port, to be called "Montagu Town". He had been made Governor of St Vincent and St Lucia in the West Indies by George I, and his plan was to send settlers and all sorts of stores to those islands, and to import from them large quantities of sugar. Unfortunately, when an expedition of seven ships, with a hundred people and ample stores, and even some sort of pre-fabricated

The Beaulieu River at Buckler's Hard.

The wide village street of Buckler's Hard.

buildings, arrived at the Islands, they had been recently occupied by the French, who politely but firmly drove the British away. Montagu Town, therefore, was abandoned, but the quay, and the road leading to it, were very useful for the timber trade, and between the 1740s and the early nineteenth century, Buckler's Hard came into its own as a centre of ship-building, both for the Navy and the Merchant Service. Between fifty and sixty naval vessels were built there, including the famous 64-gun *Agamemnon*, launched in 1781, said to have been Nelson's favourite ship, and about fifteen merchant vessels. The first builders were the brothers Wyatt, and later the very well-known ship-builder Henry Adams was put in charge by the Navy Board, and he and his descendants carried on the work until iron and steel gradually took the place of the wooden ships. Henry Adams lived in the Master Builder's House, now a hotel.

A fascinating Maritime Museum, formerly the *New Inn*, was opened in 1963 by Admiral of the Fleet the Earl Mountbatten of Burma. There is also a little chapel, which was once a cobbler's shop and believed to have been used by smugglers, and later a dame's school. Among other interesting objects in the chapel are an altar given by John, second Baron Montagu of Beaulieu, an old French statue of the Blessed Virgin Mary to whom the chaped is dedicated, and a block of wood said to have been an old chopping-block of the monks of Beaulieu.

Some ship-building is now again taking place at Buckler's Hard and, besides all the facilities for yachtsmen, there are pleasure-boats running up and down the river and to some of the Solent ports during the summer months.

Just north of Buckler's Hard is a small thatched building, Bath Cottage, built about 1760 by George, Duke of Montagu as a bathing-hut, with a pool of sea-water beside it.

Further north again is Bailey's Hard, where the Beaulieu River's very first naval vessel, the *Salisbury* of 48 guns, was built by the Herring brothers, and launched in 1698.

A little further up the river is Beaulieu, a charming village with a few pleasant old houses. The road here runs across the river, where it was partly dammed to make the monks' millpool, and there is still a tidemill. Beaulieu is famous historically for its abbey, and more recently for the National Motor Museum. The abbey, of the Cistercian Order, was founded by King John in 1204. In the Foundation Charter of 1205, King John "gave to the Church of St Mary de Bello Loco Regis which we have founded in the New Forest and to the Abbot and monks who shall serve God there the very place in which their Abbey is situated". The name "Beaulieu" was a translation into the Norman French. Quite a large area of land was granted with the abbey, and there were several granges round about, and one as far away as Faringdon, Berkshire, where the abbey had been sited for about two years, before being moved to

Beaulieu mill pool. To the right is the tide mill, in the centre the Porter's Lodge of the Abbey, and to the left the roofs of Palace House.

Beaulieu where there was more timber available. The abbey church was a magnificent building, 336 feet long and 186 feet across the transepts, the largest Cistercian church in England. It was consecrated in 1246, Henry III and other members of the court being present. Although this beautiful church was largely destroyed at the Dissolution of the Monasteries, the plan of it has been very well marked out on the ground, by the Montagu family, and several portions of the rest of the abbey remain. The south aisle wall of the church is still standing, with two doorways into the cloister court. There is also a part of the south transept wall, and in the thickness of this there was a night stairway from the monks' dormitory to the church. The chapter house was east of the cloister court, and its three beautiful entrance arches remain. The lay brothers' quarters were at the west and are still standing, being now used as a museum and a restaurant. The monks' refectory, to the south, was fortunately

58

kept complete and is now the village church, dedicated to the Blessed Virgin Mary and Child. It is in the Early English style with lancet windows, and still has a pulpit, or reader's lectern, from which a monk used to read aloud an improving book to the other monks at meal-times. There is a narrow stairway up to the pulpit, and a blocked hatch formerly leading into the kitchen.

In the south range there are also some slight remains of the monks' lavatorium (wash-hand basins), and the infirmary was east of the chapter house. The whole plan of the abbey was more like that of Clairvaux in France than that of the other English Cistercian monasteries, and it is thought to have been designed by a French architect.

Manual labour was one of the obligations of the Cistercian order, and among the occupations were agriculture, vine-growing and wine-making, sheep and cattle farming, carpentry and other timber work, wood-carving, painting and enamelling, and salt-production. A good quality of wool was produced, and sold to Italian merchants at Southampton, as well as in the home market. A building, believed to have been the winepress, remains in fairly good condition, north of where the abbey church stood. The life was very austere, but relaxations were made for monks or lay-brothers who were ill.

The entrance arches to the Chapter House of Beaulieu Abbey.

Conan Doyle, in *The White Company*, gives a good description of life at the abbey in the fourteenth century. The abbot had to provide two archers for the defence of Southampton, and several other men-at-arms in the abbey and elsewhere, to resist possible invasions. The inner gatehouse of the abbey was rebuilt in the fourteenth century, possibly as a defensive measure. The abbey had the right of sanctuary, and among well-known people who took sanctuary there were Queen Margaret of Anjou, wife of Henry VI, the Countess of Warwick, widow of the "King-Maker", and the impostor Perkin Warbeck, though he was lured away by false promises of pardon.

The abbey was dissolved early in 1538, and later in the year Henry VIII sold the house and what remained of the monastery to Thomas Wriothesley, first Earl of Southampton, already mentioned at Titchfield. Many of the stones of the abbey were used for Calshot and Hurst Castles and other defensive works.

Late in the next century, a Wriothesley, the fourth Earl of Southampton, married a Montagu, and so the connection of the Montagus with Beaulieu began. After various changes of ownership over the next two hundred years, Beaulieu came in 1865 to Lord Henry Scott, who in due course was created first Baron Montagu for services to Queen Victoria. He restored the abbey as far as possible. His son, the second Baron Montagu, was a pioneer of motoring, and took Edward VII for drives in a very early Daimler, and the present Lord Montagu, the third Baron, founded the Montagu Motor Museum in his memory.

Palace House, now the home of the Montagu family, was formerly the gatehouse of the abbey, where guests were received. It included two small parallel chapels on the first floor. It has been greatly altered, restored and enlarged by the Montagus and their ancestors in the centuries since the Dissolution, but several original features can still be seen. Many rooms are open to the public, and form a museum of beautiful furniture, portraits of the Wriothesleys and other distinguished connections of the Montagus, and various artistic and interesting relics. The outer gatehouse or porter's lodge is probably thirteenth century.

Formerly adjoining the house was the Montagu Motor Museum, which included the 1899 Daimler in which the present Prince of Wales, as well as his great-great grandfather, has driven, and which still takes part in the Veteran Cars' London-Brighton run.

In 1968 the third Baron Montagu set up a charitable trust, largely supported by the motor industry and by various individuals, to make a much larger museum, now known as the National Motor Museum, housed in magnificent new premises in the grounds. Here the whole history of the motor industry, from 1895 to the present day, can be seen. There are cars from the earliest "horseless carriages" with tiller steering to the racing cars with speeds of over 400 m.p.h., motor-cycles and commercial vehicles, models, accessories and a splendid library. In the grounds there is a monorail, in which one can ride among the tree-tops, or one can be driven round in an old London open-topped bus, from which there is an excellent view of the abbey ruins. There are also restaurants, and other facilities, including "Ladies" and "Gentlemen" written up in the languages of every likely visitor.

In the Muniment Room at Palace House have been kept the church and other village records from the Dissolution until about the middle of the nineteenth century, and in less detail events until almost the present day have been recorded. They give a most interesting picture of village life, and of how much it was governed by the church. Probably other villages, not so carefully recorded, had much the same sort of history, although Beaulieu was in a special position with regard to the abbey, even after the Dissolution. The chief officials in the early days were the churchwardens and the constable. The former had considerable power, and the latter had all sorts of duties, including that of conveying lunatics to an asylum. The churchwardens' accounts show all kinds of interesting items, some in connection with the church, but others for relief to travellers and beggars, destruction of vermin which included foxes, badgers, stoats, polecats and all sorts of birds, and providing "beer and biskit" to undertakers. People were "buried in wollens according to the law". This law was introduced when the wool trade was falling. Sometimes so many people were buried in a short time that it is probable that there was a smallpox epidemic: indeed smallpox is mentioned several times, and sometimes people might be paid a few shillings for looking after smallpox victims. There were two churches at Beaulieu before the present one, but nothing is left of them, and not much known about them. There was a school very early in the eighteenth century. Some children went into apprenticeship at the age of seven, and were not always very well treated, though the parish officials did their best to look after them.

Beaulieu Heath, south-west of the abbey, is one of the open parts of the New Forest, and is noted for the number of its barrows, or butts as they are sometimes called locally, mainly from the Bronze Age.

A few miles south of Beaulieu and Buckler's Hard is St Leonard's, a former grange of the abbey. There are the remains of a small chapel, c. 1300, with parts of its east and west windows surviving, a house, possibly of the very early eighteenth century, and a huge barn, standing within the remains of an older and more enormous one. The outer barn, of which the east gable and part of the west gable survive, was 216 feet long and 60 feet high. It is interesting to compare this old barn with the beautiful one at Great Coxwell, Faringdon, which probably belonged to the Beaulieu abbey grange there.

East gable of the great barn at St Leonard's.

Much of the Solent shore just south and west of St Leonard's is now private property, though there are a few small creeks into which boats can penetrate. The next place of interest is Sowley Pond, a very pretty little lake with wooded shores, and a little further on is Pylewell Park, with beautiful grounds open to the public on certain days in the summer.

Sowley Pond.

CHAPTER SEVEN

Lymington and the New Forest

WEST of Pylewell, the Lymington River flows out. The way in for yachts and boats is marked by The Royal Lymington Yacht Club starting platform and hut to the east, and a beacon called Jack-in-the-Basket to the west. There is marshy and muddy land, often covered by water, on both sides of the river, but the channel is clearly marked with beacons, with such picturesque names as Tar Barrel Post, Bag of Halfpence, and Cocked Hat.

"Jack in the Basket" marks the entrance to the Lymington River. In the distance can be seen the west end of the Isle of Wight and the Needles, and to the right lies Hurst Castle.

Lymington River is quite as popular with yachtsmen as Hamble River and Beaulieu River, and in the season one can hardly see the water for the vast numbers of craft moored or anchored. In contrast to the beautiful yachts are the rather ungainly-looking, but very practical, car-carrying ferries from Lymington Harbour Station to Yarmouth in the Isle of Wight. This makes a very pleasant crossing, about a third of it being along the windings of the river.

The Royal Lymington Yacht Club has a club house, and there is also a

Looking south down Lymington River. Tennyson Down, highest point of the western backbone of the Isle of Wight, is in the centre of the picture.

Lymington Town Sailing Club. Yacht-building, repairing, chandlering, racing, and every imaginable connection with yachting and boating may be found at Lymington. Three of the most famous yachts built there were the

Lymington Harbour, crowded to capacity with yachts. The town is on the left.

Arrow, *Lulworth* and *Alarm*, built between 1820 and 1830, for Mr Joseph Weld, who lived at Pylewell Park when not at the ancestral home of Lulworth Castle, Dorset. He was a noteworthy yachtsman and one of the original members of the Royal Yacht Squadron, then known simply as "The Yacht Club". The *Alarm* and *Arrow*, large and beautiful cutters, both won many races, but when challenged by *America* of the New York Yacht Club, the *Arrow* ran ashore between Ventnor and Bonchurch, and the *Alarm* stood by to help her, so they lost their chances. They were later altered to schooner rig. The *Arrow* was 85 tons, and the *Alarm* originally 193 tons. Now that sailing is so popular, among people of far more limited incomes than Joseph Weld and his friends, the Lymington shipyards turn out much smaller yachts, such as the *Contessa 32* class, very successful in the 1976 Cowes Week, and the "one-eighth-ton" class, promoted by the Lymington Town Sailing Club, also in 1976. This is the smallest size that could be built to the International Offshore Rule (I.O.R.). Among various specifications, it must have four permanent berths, an installed toilet, a minimum water supply and not more than eight sails. There are so many rules and regulations, and such a complicated terminology, about sailing, that a landsman can hardly hope to understand much about it, but everyone can enjoy watching it.

Apart from its sailing interests, Lymington is a fascinating and very historical old town. On its northern border is Buckland Rings, an Iron Age earthwork with a triple rampart, showing that there was human life in the district from very early times. Another earthwork, called Ampress Hole, may have been a Saxon dock, and also was at one time probably an oyster bed, many oyster-shells having been found there. In Norman times, Lymington was already a flourishing town. There is some disagreement among historians as to the date of its first charter as a borough, but it was probably between 1150 and 1250, so that the borough was well over seven hundred years old, possibly eight hundred when, to the grief of most of the people in the district, it was swallowed up by the New Forest District Council and ceased to be a borough. It has a new Town Hall, opened by Her Majesty Queen Elizabeth II in 1966, and it still has a Town Mayor.

The de Redvers family was the most important in Lymington in Norman times. The town was noted for ship-building from that time until the eighteenth century, and in the fourteenth century Lymington supplied twice as many ships as Portsmouth did for the wars against France. It was also a very important port for foreign trade, the river then being much less silted up than now: at one time it was considered more important than Southampton. Its other chief source of wealth was sea salt. Large salt marshes lay to the south-west of the town. Sea-water was drawn off into trenches, and from them into ponds lined with clay, where the water evaporated in the sun and wind. What was left was then piped into cisterns and boiling houses, where it was boiled over coal fires in iron or copper pans. Small wind-pumps were often used for drawing up the water. Celia Fiennes, visited Lymington towards the end of the seventeenth century, and gave an interesting account of the salterns at that date, and Daniel Defoe also mentioned the fine Lymington salt in his travel journals at the beginning of the eighteenth century, but it is thought that the business began as early as the twelfth century. When salt was almost the only preservative, it was, of course, of immense value, and Lymington salt was sold all over the south and other parts of England and to the ships, and was exported to foreign countries. Unfortunately, in the nineteenth century, a heavy salt tax and a heavy coal tax took away most of the profits, and in addition, rock salt from Cheshire and thereabouts, which could easily be transported by train when the railways started, became a serious rival, and the Lymington salterns practically ceased to exist. Very little remains of them, and what there is is used for other purposes.

Lymington, like most other towns, had occasional outbreaks of the plague, and a mayor died of it in 1611. During the Civil War, Lymington's sympathies seem to have been largely Parliamentarian. Readers who enjoyed Captain Marryat's *Children of the New Forest* will remember that Jacob Armitage, the old forester who took in the Beverley children after the

Roundheads had destroyed their house, Arnewood, by fire, did his shopping and sold his venison in Lymington. He must have been careful to conceal his Royalist sympathies. To turn from fiction to fact, a Captain St Barbe raised a troop of horses for the Parliament, and many soldiers were lodged in the town. Some of these, perhaps surprisingly for so-called Puritans, were described as "disorderly, lewde and lawless". They defaced the parish church, St Thomas, and the churchyard. Fortunately the town records had been sent to Hurst Castle for safe keeping.

Some Lymingtonians were Royalists, and in 1648 the mayor, Bernard Knapton and some others joined in an unsuccessful attempt by Prince Charles to rescue Charles I. After the restoration, the Royal Arms of Charles II was put up in the church, but when George I came to the throne the letter 'C' was changed to 'G', as an economy measure.

At the time of the Monmouth Rebellion, in 1685, an ex-mayor, Thomas Dore, raised a troop of horse for the Duke of Monmouth, and his supporters met in Mrs Knapton's house, Monmouth House, a very fine house still standing in the High Street and now a nursing home.

In the next century, there were several Royal visits. Frederick Prince of Wales, father of George III, lived for a time at Pylewell Park, and George III visited the well-known Lymington family, the Burrard Neales, at Wallhampton, on the east bank of the Lymington River. The borough had two members of Parliament from the time of Elizabeth I until the second Reform Bill, and one of the members in the eighteenth century was Edward Gibbon, of *Decline and Fall of the Roman Empire* fame. At about this time, too, Lymington was well known as a health resort, and a Mrs Beeston ran some "strengthening sea baths".

General Wolfe spent his last night in England at Lymington, and a British fleet assembled in Lymington Harbour before sailing for the victory of Quiberon Bay.

During the French Revolution, several French emigrés came to Lymington, and some were lodged in the picturesque old Malt House. This, with some carefully done alterations and extensions, is now used as a Community Centre. It was started soon after the 1939-45 war by Mr Hole, a pioneer of these excellent institutions.

Many books have been written about Lymington, and from *Literary Recollections* written by the Reverend Richard Warner in 1776, we learn that Lymington "had a moral and social beauty which, though not then exclusively its own, was generally acknowledged to be more conspicuous there, than in most other places". The young ladies, it seems, were absolute paragons of virtue and beauty, and the people in general avoided the pernicious habit of late dinner, and usually dined at 2 o'clock, or 3 o'clock at the latest, thereby keeping their excellent health and their country complexions.

In addition to its moral excellence Lymington was, and still is, a charming town architecturally. The High Street, with many good Georgian

The lower end of Lymington High Street.

and some earlier houses, slopes steeply down hill towards the quay. At the top stands the Church of St Thomas the Apostle, which was restored in due course after the ravages of the Parliamentarians. It is thought to have been built on the site of an earlier, Norman church. The chancel, and the north, or Courtenay, Chapel, built by Hugh Courtenay, Earl of Devon, as a mortuary chapel c. 1325, are mainly Early English. The base of the tower is late Norman. The upper part was added c. 1670, and is topped by a cupola added in Georgian times. There are also Georgian galleries, and some fifteenth century roof bosses have been preserved in a glass case. Among interesting

The Church of St Thomas the Apostle, at the top end of Lymington High Street. The house on the right, with its mantle of creeper, is known as Wistaria House.

memorials is a Rysbrack bust to Charles Colborne, 1747, and one by John Bacon, R.A. to Captain Josias Rogers, R.N., 1795, who was born in Lymington in 1755 and had an extraordinarily adventurous career in the War of American Independence and also in the wars against France. He died of yellow fever, to the extreme grief of his crew, who adored him. His friend the Reverend Richard Warner wrote, "the tear of conscious and irretrievable bereavement rolled down the furrowed cheek of many a brave and thoughtless tar".

Along the quay and in the streets near it there are a great many picturesque houses, and a sea-water bath house of the early nineteenth century. On the quay, not far from the Yacht Club, stands a handsome gas-lamp on a Doric column, with an inscription "of respect and gratitude" to Admiral Sir H. Burrard Neale, for a "munificent gift" of iron columns for Lymington's first gas lamps in 1832. Another memorial to him is a column, of the Cleopatra's Needle type, on Wallhampton Hill across the harbour.

The motto under Lymington's coat-of-arms is "Twixt Sea and Forest Enchanted", and certainly Lymington is one of the best places on the Solent from which to approach the New Forest. Though called "New", the Forest has in fact been inhabited from the Old Stone Age, and was only known as "New" when William the Conqueror made new laws about hunting. The laws were extremely severe, and made the Norman kings and their followers very unpopular, but it has now long been realised that they did not commit nearly all the crimes attributed to them, did not destroy any churches or villages, and did not spoil much agricultural land, for which the greater part of the Forest was in any case unsuited. Although the Forest inhabitants were not allowed to

69

hunt, they had, and still have, many common rights such as "estovers" and "turbary", wood and turf fuel respectively, "pasture rights" for cattle, sheep and horses, and "pannage" for pigs in the autumn, when they can eat acorns and beech-mast. The domestic and wild animals wandering about in the Forest form one of its great attractions, the ponies with their foals being particularly charming. Deer and other wild animals can sometimes be seen. In some parts of the Forest there are official car parks and camping grounds, but it is still quite easy to leave the beaten tracks and to walk or ride for hours without seeing anything modern.

Parts of the Forest are open heath-land, some standing quite high with fine views; others are woods of the most beautiful beeches, oaks and birches, and others of coniferous trees. In some places there are "arboreta" of exotic trees such as redwoods, planted in the nineteenth century. Masses of rhododendrons, and of gorse and heather in their seasons, form brilliant patches of colour. In the little valleys or "bottoms" there are fascinating little streams, and the whole area is of indescribable beauty.

There is much history attached to some of the villages. The Church of St Peter, Brockenhurst, about a quarter of a mile outside the village, is one of two Forest churches mentioned in the Domesday Survey, and the Norman nave survives. The chancel is thirteenth century, and there are additions from later dates. In the churchyard is one of those enormous yew trees which are a feature of Hampshire, and there is a tombstone to "Brusher" Mills, a nineteenth century New Forest character who earned his living by the rather curious occupation of catching adders. There are still many of these in the forest, but in general they seem to avoid humans as much as humans avoid them.

Lyndhurst, the capital of the Forest, has a beautiful house known as the Queen's House or King's House, according to who occupies the throne at the

The Queen's House and St Michael's Church at Lyndhurst.

moment. Much of this is seventeenth century, but there was a house there from much earlier times, and kings and queens used to stay there. The Forest had, and still to some extent has, its own laws and officers, verderers, agisters and others, and the courts were held in the Queen's House. The church, St Michael, on the site of a former classical one, is Victorian, and full of treasures of the Pre-Raphaelite period, such as windows by Morris and Burne-Jones, and a reredos of the wise and foolish virgins by Lord Leighton. The grave of Mrs Hargreaves, the original of "Alice in Wonderland" is in the churchyard.

Foxlease, the famous Girl Guide Officers' Training School, adjoins

 Beech and fir woods in the New Forest.

Lyndhurst. It is a pleasant eighteenth century house, and has some beautiful "Strawberry Hill Gothic" rooms.

Minstead, north of Lyndhurst, has a fascinating church, originally thirteenth century, and with a twelfth century font, but is remarkable mainly for its profusion of eighteenth century galleries, including a private one with a fireplace, and its three-decker pulpit.

Towards the Lymington end of the Forest, in the parish of Hordle, and somewhere near where the Beverleys' house, Arnewood, must be supposed to have stood, is a remarkable erection called Peterson's Tower, or sometimes Peterson's Folly. Peterson was a judge of the High Court at Calcutta, and when he retired and went to live at Arnewood, he erected a concrete tower, 218 feet high, partly to show his belief in concrete, and partly to ameliorate local unemployment, which was then prevalent. Those who had called it Peterson's Folly were confounded, for it is still standing, a thin, gaunt tower in the Indian style of architecture. When Peterson had completed the tower, he fixed a lamp at the top of it, but, as this confused the crews of ships in the Solent, the Admiralty told him to extinguish it, and never to light it again. When Peterson died, his ashes, at his own wish, were deposited at the bottom of the tower, but when the Peterson property was sold, they were dug up and transferred to Sway churchyard, to his wife's grave. He had been a Spiritualist, and believed that the spirit of Sir Christopher Wren had inspired his building of the tower.

So many books have been written about the New Forest, that it needs no further description here. It has an area of about 250 square miles, and has so many attractions that several days could be spent there before returning to Lymington and the Solent proper.

Peterson's Tower, near Hordle, can be seen from far up the Solent and well out into the Channel.

CHAPTER EIGHT

Woodside to Mudeford

WHERE the Lymington salterns used to be are the hamlets of Woodside and Lower Pennington. At Woodside one of the old salt boiling houses can still be seen, and there is an inn, the *Chequers*, partly made from the timbers of a French fishing boat, *Le Hareng Rouge*, about which there is an extraordinary "cautionary tale". At one time winkles flourished in the Solent, especially between Needs Oar Point and Hurst Castle. Many families made their living by winkle fishing, but in the last quarter of the nineteenth century French boats poached the greater part of the winkle harvest. The French method of winkling was to blow a special whistle which attracted the winkles and led them to climb on to rush mats hung over the gunwales. The *Hareng Rouge* had the bad luck to come into contact with a winkle migration. This took place every year, when millions of winkles migrated to more westerly waters, but in this particular year they were earlier than usual, on account of a warm season. When, therefore, the French whistles were blown, instead of a reasonable catch of winkles, they attracted hundreds of thousands of the creatures, which climbed up the mats and into the boat at such speed that the crew could not keep up with clearing the mats, and eventually there was such a weight of winkles on board that the boat sank with all hands. Some poachers, at least, must have been put off by this dreadful fate.

One of the few reminders of the former salt industry round Lymington, a boiling house at Woodside.

Another shell-fish which flourished in the Solent was the oyster. British oysters were known and appreciated by the Romans and there have always been oyster beds at various places round the coast of Britain. Even though some of the monks of Winchester ate oysters as Lenten fare, they have generally been looked on as a luxury food, and Solent oysters were considered some of the best in the nineteenth century, when the Solent was still very little polluted. Unluckily, in spite of the comparatively clean waters, the Solent oysters caught a devastating disease, and the industry was temporarily wiped out. It has been revived of late years, from Calshot right along to Poole. The heavy pollution of the Solent now makes the oysters unsafe for eating, but they are very valuable for breeding purposes, and are exported in great quantities, not only to other British oyster beds but also to the Continent.

There are some pleasant walks about this part of the Solent shore, and Pennington Marshes form a happy hunting ground for ornithologists. Uncommon, and even very rare birds, are seen there from time to time, specially in the migratory season. Near the marshes is a little island, about 500 yards by 50 yards at high tide, which is a nesting place of Little Terns, among other interesting birds, and this is looked after by a warden and helpers.

Just to the west of the marshes and the former salterns is Keyhaven. The name is said to come from the Saxon word "cy-haefenn", "the harbour where cows were shipped", so it must have been a little port from early times. Now it is another popular yachting harbour, with its own yacht club, quay, hard and

Sailing at Keyhaven.

Fishermen at Keyhaven.

boat-yard. Sometimes the harbour is full of swans, as beautiful a sight as when it is full of yachts. The most navigable channel from Keyhaven to Hurst Point is called "Keyhaven Lake", "Lake" being a common name for quite narrow channels of water round the Solent. At high tide the marshy land all round is covered with water, and navigation has to be undertaken carefully.

At Keyhaven there is a pleasant old inn called *The Gun*, with a real, very old gun, possibly dredged up from the sea, on top of its front porch. A part of the lounge is known as "The Chapel Bar" and it is thought that drowned corpses may sometimes have been brought in there, and a clergyman summoned to say prayers over them. When the melancholy tasks had been accomplished, refreshment could be taken in the public bar a few yards away.

A ferry runs from Keyhaven to Hurst Castle in the summer months. Hurst Point has two lighthouses, the High Light and the Low Light. This is the narrowest part of the Solent, the distance to Cliff End, the nearest point on the Isle of Wight, being only about a mile. It looks as if a strong swimmer could

The Gun Inn at Keyhaven.

easily manage the crossing, but, in fact, there are very strong and dangerous currents, and sensible swimmers do not attempt it.

Hurst Castle (open daily to public from May until September and at other times by arrangement) was another of Henry VIII's coast defences. It was built between 1541 and 1544, and in 1545 a Master Gunner was appointed, at the rate of 6d. per day. The Castle had a garrison of 25 men. Two of these forts, Hurst Castle on the mainland and Yarmouth Castle in the Isle of Wight, command the west entrance to the Solent where it is narrowest. Hurst Castle is situated at the end of a spit of shingle jutting out towards the

Isle of Wight. It consists of a central tower, twelve-sided externally, with two floors and a basement. It is surrounded by a curtain wall on which there are three semi-circular bastions, on the north-west, north-east and south. Only the north-west bastion remains as it must have looked when first built, the rest having been much rebuilt. In the room over the gateway is the portcullis, which still retains its weights and chains. In the basement is a circular room, in the centre of which is a large brick pier which contains a staircase leading to the roof. It also supports the brick vaulting of the ceiling of the basement.

Hurst Castle. The Henry VIII fortification is towards the left.

Hurst Castle from an old print, c.1850.

The stonework of this castle was obtained largely from Beaulieu Abbey. Although the demolition of the abbey church was a shocking architectural loss, Henry considered that he had some excuse for it, because the country was menaced by enemies, and there was plenty of wood and stone lying about for the taking, to speed up the building of the castle while the crisis lasted. However, as time passed, the atmosphere grew less hectic, and the gun platforms were allowed to fall into a state of decay. When the castle gunners were ordered to stop some Flemish ships in 1589 and 1593, they were unable to do so.

During the Civil War, the castle was occupied by the Parliamentary forces, and it was then that it came most noticeably into our national history. King Charles I, having been imprisoned for a year at Carisbrooke Castle on the Isle of Wight, was brought to Hurst Castle by the Army on 30th November 1648. When the king asked to which castle he was being conducted and heard that it was Hurst, he said, "You could not have named a worse," and he was probably right. From a contemporary account by Sir Thomas Herbert, we learn that the king was "slenderly accommodated". The room which he used as a dining room needed candles even at noonday during December, and "the air was noxious by reason of the unwholsom vapours arising from the weeds the salt water casts upon the shore and by the fogs that these marine places are most subject to". The castle was also described as standing "a mile and a half in the sea, upon a beach full of mud and stinking ooze upon low tides, having no fresh water within two or three miles of it, so cold, boggy and noisome that the guards cannot endure it without shifting quarters". The king was kept in this dreary spot for nineteen days, after which he was taken to Windsor, where he spent a very lonely Christmas, and thence to London and his execution on 30th January 1649.

Hurst Castle continued on the active list until Victorian times, when two large wings were added to it, on the east and west (1873). In 1933, having become obsolete, it was handed over by the War Office to the Office of Works (now Department of the Environment). The nation, however, had not yet dispensed with it, as it was occupied again by the services during the Second World War. Since then, it has once more been relegated to its former role of ancient monument.

From Hurst Castle, a shingle bank, Hurst Beach, runs westward. This makes a very scenic, if hard-to-the-feet, walk of rather over a mile, with a beautiful view of the Island and the Needles on one side, and the Keyhaven marshes on the other. At the north-west end of it, a footbridge leads to a road, sometimes impassable at high tide, leading in one direction to Keyhaven, past the hamlet of Saltgrass, and in the other to Milford-on-Sea. Walkers can go on to Milford by the shore, with Sturt Pond, also at one time connected with the salterns, on the right: this is a wide stretch of water fed by the Dane Stream, and flowing out as a wide stream between the shingle bank and the marshes.

Milford was a hamlet mentioned in the Domesday Survey, and a few old relics such as chipped flints suggest that there may have been a settlement there long before Norman times. "Church land at Melleford" was mentioned in the Forest Survey of the Domesday Book, showing that the Forest must have extended further south in those days than it does now. The name derives from an old mill, which still exists, but is not in private hands and has not been in use for some time.

The church, All Saints, is largely Early English, but it is on the site of a former Norman one, and possibly of a Saxon one before that. It still has Norman arches in the south arcade of the west end of the nave, and small Norman doorways at the ends of the transepts. The tower, at the west end, was built in the early thirteenth century, and its octagonal, lead spire probably added in the fourteenth century. A curious feature of the outside of the tower is that it has two "lean-to" extensions against the lower part of its north and south walls. These were probably prolongations of the Norman aisles. They each have a lancet window in the west wall, and a low, pointed arch leading into the tower, and there were possibly archways, now bricked up, leading into the nave. The chancel is good Early English of about 1260, and the windows show the beginnings of tracery. In the north window of the chancel is a figure of Charles I, with his crown at his feet and a halo round his head, and a martyr's palm in his right hand. The inscription is "Carolus Rex et M." and at the bottom of the window is the one word "Remember". Charles said this to Bishop Juxon, who was at his side until the moment of the execution: it does not seem to be known what the Bishop was to remember. Hurst Castle is in the parish of Milford, so it is appropriate that this window should be in Milford Church, though Parliamentary supporters would doubtless not agree.

All Saints Church, Milford-on-Sea, with the curious "lean-to" extensions against the tower.

79

The ceiling of the chancel, the crossing and transepts and the east bay of the nave is Jacobean, c. 1640, and has timber crossing ribs with good bosses, restored to their original colours of recent years. At the west end of the south aisle is a large picture, by Perugino or one of his school, given by one of the Cornwallis-West family in memory of his father. There is a row of amusing grotesques round the outside of the top of the tower, and on a window of the south aisle, just east of the porch, a comic figure of a man playing bagpipes, and evidently finding it a considerable effort.

Much of the income of Milford, as of Lymington, came from the salterns, and it was quite a prosperous village, though small, until the decline of the salt industry. In the 1860s the character of the village was considerably changed by the Cornwallis-Wests, who occupied Newlands Manor, a nineteenth century Gothic mansion on a 2,000 acre estate just north of Milford. There was a plan to make Milford into a large sea-side resort, with a railway station, a pier and bandstand, pleasure gardens, a hotel and a hydro. The "on-Sea" part of the name was added at that time. The hotel was, in fact, built, and gardens developed to a certain extent in the valley of the Dane stream, but the rest of the scheme collapsed for want of capital. Part of the village remained, and still does, as it has always been, but many new houses were built, some of them being quite handsome, with large gardens. In Edwardian days, Newlands Manor was much frequented by the aristocracy, visitors including Edward VII himself and the Kaiser.

Since the end of the First World War, there has been an enormous growth of housing. Small houses and bungalows have sprung up at the east end of the village and up at the back, and of late years most of the Victorian and Edwardian houses on Hordle Cliff, at the west end of the village, have been demolished, and hundreds of flats put up in their places, so that the character of the place has quite changed. Newlands Manor has been turned into luxury flats. The shore, however, is not much spoiled. It has a background of sandy cliffs, then a shingle bank and, at low tide, good sands. In the summer, Milford-on-Sea is too crowded to be altogether enjoyable, but in the winter the shore is often deserted except for a few patient fishermen, and residents exercising their dogs. There are lovely views of the Isle of Wight to the south-east, and of Hengistbury Head and, further on, the Purbeck Hills to the west, and one can forget the modern buildings.

Cliff erosion is a serious problem all along this part of the Solent shore, and no very effective way of combating it seems to have been yet discovered, though research is always going on.

The railway station for Milford-on-Sea is New Milton, three or four miles away. Unlike the New Forest, New Milton really is comparatively new, having grown up mainly since the opening of the railway from Brockenhurst to Bournemouth in the 1880s. Before that, it had not been considered necessary for Christchurch or Bournemouth to have railway stations, and horse-drawn coaches were run from Holmsley Station on the now-demolished line to Ringwood but, with Bournemouth's enormous expansion, the London and South Western Railway decided to open a line from Brockenhurst via Christchurch. Milton, being on the direct line, had its station opened in 1886. It is said that the name "New Milton" was taken from the "new" Milton Post Office, in a little group of houses near the railway, Milton Post Office being then in what is now known as Old Milton. In the early twentieth century, a steam bus conveyed passengers to and from the station. Before the coming of the railway, Milton (the "middle town" between Christchurch and Lymington) was a tiny village. Now, with its seaside neighbour Barton-on-Sea, it is an ever-increasing town, with over 18,000 inhabitants. It has not many interesting buildings, but a few remain from the old days. Fernhill Manor, north of the railway, and now a girls' school, is partly a handsome late seventeenth century building, on the site of a much earlier manor. Little Gore Farm, in Gore Road ("Gore" in this connection meaning a triangular piece of land) is an old farmhouse with old barns, and in it is a very old lead pump, ornamented with a coat-of-arms. The land about here formerly belonged to Christchurch Priory, and was all agricultural land, but now the very few old buildings that are left are all mixed up in housing estates and small factory developments, and there is a vast new school and Adult Education Centre, called Arnewood.

Captain Marryat, who wrote *Mr. Midshipman Easy* and several other excellent books as well as *The Children of the New Forest*, lived for some time at Chewton Glen, now a luxury hotel, a very attractive house in large grounds at the west end of New Milton parish. Opposite Chewton Glen is a huge, permanent caravan park, and innumerable holiday chalets, so that visitors of any standard of income can enjoy their holidays in this delightful district.

Milton church, St Mary Magdalene, has an early seventeenth century tower, but the rest is nineteenth century brick, with twentieth century additions in a modern Georgian style. In the porch is a good marble monument to Thos. White, 1720, a bewigged soldier in armour, who "served Three Kings and Queen Anne as a Commander in Ye Guards" in wars in Ireland and Flanders, "and was much wounded". He has a sword in one hand and a helmet in the other, and a real, contemporary sword in a case hangs down by the monument. Over the church door there are two very attractive cherub heads. Near the pulpit there is a piece of tracery from a very much earlier church.

In the eighteenth century, Milton was a centre for smuggling. Chewton Bunny and Beckton Bunny ("Bunny" being the local name for a wooded valley leading down to the sea), at different ends of the parish, both being much used by smugglers. In 1780 they murdered a Customs Officer at Milton, but by the middle of the nineteenth century the district had become very respectable, and had begun to attract visitors.

Barton-on-Sea was much frequented by geologists. The cliffs there, geologically known as Upper Bagshot or Barton Beds, were noted for fossils. The remains of a crocodile, and hundreds of different species of sea-shells, have been found there, and bones of reptiles and mammals have also been found in the beds of clay in Hordle Cliffs, just east of Barton. Many fossils can still be found, though probably some of the best were discovered in the nineteenth century. At the top of the cliffs is the golf links, a very sporting and exciting course, from which it must sometimes be tempting to keep one's eye on the view instead of on the ball. Barton is almost entirely residential. In the middle of it there is a memorial column commemorating Indian soldiers who stayed in a convalescent home set up for them there during the 1914-18 war. The column has inscriptions in their languages on the sides, and in English on the front.

Highcliffe, a very large residential village and seaside resort, is the next place westward on the Solent shore. Even if the cliffs there are a little higher than those of Milford and Barton, there are quite easy slopes down to the shore, where there are good sands for the children. Until the eighteenth century this was an almost uninhabited part of the coast, but in 1773 the third Earl of Bute who, for a short time, had been a rather unsuccessful Prime Minister to George III, had a large house built there by Robert Adam. At first it was called High Cliff, but later the name was changed to Highcliffe Castle. Bute was much happier in country pursuits than in politics, and at High Cliff he studied botany, geology, and the natural history of the district, including the New Forest. The house, however, was expensive to maintain, and cliff erosion was a constant problem, so Bute's son Charles Stuart, to whom he left the house, had it demolished, and went to live at Bure Homage, a mile or two away. His son, another Charles, had loved Highcliffe Castle and its beautiful position, and he decided to rebuild the place, a little further back from the cliff edge. He was a successful diplomat, and was British Ambassador in Paris from about 1815 until 1830. He admired everything French, and had the new Highcliffe Castle built in the French medieval Gothic style. It included a magnificent portico on the north side, looking like the entrance to a cathedral, and leading into a large hall with hammer-beam roof, angel corbels and stained-glass windows. On the south side facing the sea, he introduced a beautiful oriel window with delicate tracery, and rows of sculptured figures playing musical instruments just under it. This, with other parts of the stonework, came from a sixteenth century manor-house at Les Andelys in Normandy, which was being demolished in 1820, just when Sir Charles Stuart was planning Highcliffe Castle. Some other parts of the stonework are pieces of medieval sculpture, believed to have come from the ruined Abbey of Jumiéges, also in Normandy.

Highcliffe Castle.

In 1828 Sir Charles was made a Baron, and chose for himself the French-sounding title of Lord Stuart de Rothesay. He built the present Highcliffe church, (Church of England), St Mark's. After his death, his daughter the Marchioness of Waterford lived in the castle for part of each year, and entertained many royal and aristocratic visitors, some of whom used to sail across in the Royal Yacht from Osborne. Edward VII as Prince of Wales was one of the visitors, and the Kaiser rented the castle for some time. Gordon Selfridge, founder of the famous firm, was another lessee of the castle. He lived at Highcliffe for some time, and when he died, he was buried in St Mark's churchyard.

Unfortunately the Stuart de Rothesay family was finally obliged to sell the castle. For a time it was a Children's Home, and then for a few years a Seminary of Claretian Monks, but after they left it remained empty, and has since been much injured by vandals, and twice suffered from fires. However, the beautiful shell of it still remains and, in 1977, strenuous efforts were being made to preserve it, and the grounds were opened to the public in honour of the Queen's Silver Jubilee.

Down on the shore, between Highcliffe and Avon Beach, Mudeford, there is a curious erection, looking just like a giant golf-ball, belonging to the Ministry of Defence Signals and Research Department.

On the main road leading down from Highcliffe to Mudeford, now a large residential area, stands the lodge of Bure Homage, the charming old farmhouse which was taken by the Earl of Bute's son, but unfortunately the house itself has been demolished.

Mudeford, between Highcliffe and Christchurch, has some delightful old houses interspersed with modern developments. Between the village and the old quay there is a large marshy area, much favoured by sea-birds, but covered with water at high tide. In 1784, a notable battle between smugglers and Customs officials took place at Mudeford Quay. The mouth of the river had long been used as a landing-place for contraband, but the smugglers had usually been careful to be unobserved. Often they dropped the casks overboard, and strong swimmers towed them to a safe landing-place, but on this occasion the smugglers seem to have been careless, and to have landed their cargo quite openly on Mudeford beach. Somehow the Customs officials, stationed at Yarmouth, Isle of Wight, got wind of this, and sailed across in H.M.S. *Orestes* to arrest the smugglers. Customers of the *Haven Inn*, thinking that they would be deprived of their cheap contraband liquor, opened fire on the Customs men, and the smugglers also ran into the *Haven* and started firing from the windows. The *Orestes* then opened fire in return, and there was a brisk exchange, during which a cannonball went down the inn chimney. The landlord, however, deciding that the better part of valour was discretion, and that it was hardly worth while having his whole inn destroyed for the sake of cheaper brandy, hung out a white flag and surrendered. After this incident, the smugglers became more cautious again.

The quay stands where the Hampshire Avon and the Dorset Stour, which join together just below Christchurch, flow out into Christchurch Bay. There is not, and was not, so far as is known, a muddy ford there, although the name is so pronounced: it is thought to come from the Saxon "muda", a river mouth. There are, however, ferries to take passengers across to the bathing beach, on the opposite bank, and to Hengistbury Head. The Highcliffe Sailing Club has its club house on Mudeford Quay, and the Mudeford Yacht Club at Fisherman's Bank.

George III once visited Mudeford, in 1803, on his way to Weymouth, and there was some idea of making it into a really large watering-place, but this did not happen, and so it has kept much of its charm. Coleridge and Sir Walter Scott both stayed at Mudeford, and Scott wrote part of *Marmion* there.

The church was built in the second half of the nineteenth century by the Ricardo family. In the spring there is a special service for fishermen, followed by the Blessing of the Waters from a boat.

Between Mudeford and Christchurch, on the bank of the river, is Stanpit Marsh, a 150-acre Nature Reserve, approached by a footpath. This marsh is another paradise for botanists and bird-watchers. The flora is typical of salt-marshes, and over 200 species of birds have been recorded there, including some quite rare ones. Considering, indeed, the almost terrifying growth of housing and factory development along the Hampshire side of the Solent, it is remarkable what a wealth of wild life is still to be found. Fortunately there is a very active Solent Protection Society, and also many other societies and individuals, to see that the wild life is well protected.

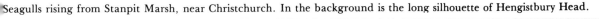

Seagulls rising from Stanpit Marsh, near Christchurch. In the background is the long silhouette of Hengistbury Head.

CHAPTER NINE

Christchurch, Hengistbury, Bournemouth and Poole

CHRISTCHURCH, formerly in Hampshire, but in Dorset since 1972, is one of the most beautiful and historical small towns in Wessex. It dates back to at least A.D. 900, and was at that time called Twynham, meaning a town between two rivers, the Avon, which runs into it from Hampshire to the north, and the Stour, which comes in from Dorset to the west. It was mentioned in the *Anglo-Saxon Chronicle*, and one Saxon writer said that Ethelwold took it from Edward the Elder in about 900. It is believed that there was already a minster church, named Christchurch, and some time later the name of the town was changed from Twynham to Christchurch. The Old Mill, mentioned in the Domesday Survey, is also said to have dated originally from Saxon times.

The road leading into Christchurch from Mudeford crosses three bridges over the Avon. From the second one there is a wonderful view of largely Norman buildings, the Constable's House, the castle keep and the Priory Church. The Constable's House, late twelfth century, is one of the best surviving examples of Norman domestic architecture in England. It is built mainly of Purbeck marble blocks. It is 67 feet by 23 feet and consisted of one large hall with a basement. It has a round window in the south wall, and some two-light windows in the other walls with zig-zag mouldings, and on the east side, by the mill-stream, there is a garde-robe tower, and a fireplace with its original flue and round chimney-stack. The castle keep, standing on a mound or "motte", is probably of a rather later date. It was built for the de Redvers family, who had been granted the church and town by Henry I. The third bridge, of two arches with very old bases, crosses a little branch of the Avon serving as a mill-stream. A path, Convent Walk, runs by the side of the stream to a little bridge known as the Norman Bridge, and by this is Place Mill, which was in use for hundreds of years.

The view of the Priory Church from the bridge includes the best piece of exterior Norman work, the stair-turret, with three rows of arcades, and some unusual trellis-work between the top and second rows.

There is an old legend about the original Saxon church. Plans were made to build it on St Catherine's Hill, a little further inland, but every night the work done during the day was undone, apparently by some supernatural

Christchurch Priory and Norman House, seen from the bridge over the Avon.

The keep of Christchurch Castle, on its artificial mound. To the right is the gable of the Norman House.

agency, and the materials moved to the present site. This being accepted as a Divine revelation, the work was started again, and all went well except that one beam was too short. An unknown workman, believed by some people to have been Christ the Carpenter, lengthened the beam to the required size during one night. This "miraculous beam" is still shown in the Priory Church, lending colour to this picturesque legend even if not, perhaps, proving its truth.

The building of the present Priory Church started towards the end of the eleventh century. William Rufus granted the church and town to Ranulph Flambard, and he built the splendid Norman nave which still exists. Other Norman work includes parts of the transepts, the crossing, which probably formerly supported a tower believed to have collapsed, or perhaps to have been demolished as unsafe, some time in the fifteenth century, some small windows and three crypts. The huge porch is magnificent Early English, and so is the clerestory above the Norman triforium in the nave. The tower, now at the west end, is fifteenth century Perpendicular. The Chancel and Lady Chapel are also Perpendicular.

Behind the High Altar is a stone reredos, c. 1350 (partly restored), in the middle of which is the reclining figure of Jesse, with David and Solomon on either side of him, and the "stem" in the form of a pillar and a vine, leading up from him to the Infant Christ. Other scenes from Christ's nativity are included. There are carved oak stalls, with "misericorde" seats, and several chantry chapels, the most beautiful being that of Margaret, Countess of Salisbury. These chantries usually included the tomb of the person whose memorial they were, and priests said masses for their souls, but in this case the chantry chapel has no occupant. The Countess of Salisbury's son, Cardinal Pole, disputed Henry VIII's right to call himself Head of the Church, and Margaret herself was known to support the Pope, so Henry had her put into the Tower of London, and beheaded and buried there, at the age of over seventy, in 1541. This chantry has beautiful fan-vaulting and delicate stone-carving by Torrigiano. Other chantries include those of Sir William Berkeley, c. 1490, and the Draper Chantry, c. 1529. John Draper was the last prior of the Augustinian priory, which had been founded in Christchurch in 1150. It came to an end in 1539, at the Dissolution, and nearly all the monastic buildings were destroyed, but the town was allowed to keep the church. John Draper, who was respected in the town and also had friends at Court, was allowed to retire on a pension and to live in comfort, but probably, when he died, no priest said masses in his chantry, as this had been forbidden.

Among interesting monuments is an alabaster one to Sir John and Lady Chydioke, 1455 and, under the tower, a white marble one to Shelley by the sculptor H. Weekes, R.A., 1854. Shelley was drowned off the Italian coast in 1822: the memorial shows his drowned figure on the knees of a mourning woman, and the verse from his poem "Adonais", beginning "He has outsoared the shadow of our night" is under it. The memorial had been offered to Westminster Abbey, but had been refused partly because it was too much like a "pieta", and partly because of Shelley's agnostic views. It was presented to Christchurch Priory by Shelley's son, who lived for some time at Boscombe.

Most of the good old houses in Christchurch are near the Priory, and in Quay Road is the Red House Museum, originally built in the early eighteenth century as a workhouse for the "comfortable support of the numerous poor of the parish of Christchurch". It is certainly not at all one's idea of a workhouse, being a charming old house with a pretty garden, and one hopes that the "numerous poor" were happy as well as comfortable. It is now a most fascinating museum of the history and pre-history of Christchurch and the district, from the Old Stone Age up to the present time. It includes natural history and geology, cottage industries, domestic objects and furniture, clothes, toys and dolls, and everything to show how people have lived through the ages. There is also an excellent library of local history, started by the Druitt family, whose collections were the foundation of the museum, and an art gallery where exhibitions are frequently held.

Christchurch Quay lies just south of the Priory, where the Stour and Avon meet. Motor-boat trips run from the quay to Mudeford and Hengistbury, and there is plenty of sailing, and rowing for people who like to be active on the water. The Christchurch Sailing Club, over one hundred years old, has its club-house on the quay, and there is a rowing club a little way up the Stour.

The stretch of water between the quay and Mudeford is called "The Run", and this is one of the best places for catching the famous Christchurch salmon. Fishing is one of the main sports, as well as industries, of the Christchurch district. Besides the salmon, there are chub, dace, perch, roach and barbel, and other fresh-water fish, and the salt-water fish include plaice, bass, flounder, bream, mackerel, conger-eel, and sometimes more exotic fish such as sharks. There is a Christchurch and District Fishing Club, which holds many competitions. Fishing is a feature of much of the Solent area, but Christchurch is perhaps the most noted and popular centre, and visiting anglers need to make their arrangements well in advance.

The bathing-beach for Christchurch, and a colony of holiday chalets, are at Mudeford Sandbank, just across the river from Mudeford Quay. These can be approached by boat from Christchurch Quay, a charming run down the river, or by a footpath on the west bank of the river, or by road to the west of Christchurch, crossing the river Stour at Tuckton Bridge and turning left by Broadway. By this last way, cars can only go as far as the west end of Hengistbury Head, and the rest of the journey has to be done on foot, or in a comic little "Noddy Train" which takes passengers and their luggage along at the back of the headland to the chalets.

Hengistbury Head, jutting out between Christchurch Bay and Poole Bay, appears from some maps to be the westward end of the north Solent coast, although other maps put it further back, at Hurst Castle. However that may be, it is certain that no-one staying in the Solent district should fail to visit Hengistbury, as it is one of the most fascinating places in the whole area.

It is not a very high headland, but stands up quite impressively, with the sea to the south and east of it, and Christchurch Harbour to the north. The highest part of it is called Warren Hill. The River Stour in early days, possibly about ten thousand years ago, flowed out into the sea to the west of Warren Hill, and it was some time later that the Stour changed its course, broke through a ridge and joined the Avon where Christchurch Quay is now. Some of the gravel and shingle deposits washed down in the original course of the Stour still form part of the beach between Hengistbury and Southbourne (the eastern part of Bournemouth). The geology of the Head is fascinating. Besides the deposits and terraces of gravel which may be anything between ten thousand and two hundred thousand years old, there are deposits, which can be well seen from the beach below Warren Hill, dating back perhaps thirty million years. These include flints, and large iron boulders called "doggers", and these hard stones have been very useful in saving the Head from being washed away. Fossils are not very frequent, though there are a few fossil tree-trunks and some sharks' teeth and vertebrae.

Human life seems to have existed on the headland on and off from the Old Stone Age until Roman times. About eleven thousand years ago there was a camp of reindeer hunters on Warren Hill: they made tools of flint and reindeer antlers. The Middle Stone Age people, c. 7,000-3,300 B.C., made bows and arrows and more advanced tools, and the New Stone Age people, c. 3,300-1500 B.C., who lived both on Warren Hill and in the lower land round about, kept sheep and cattle and grew wheat. They also traded with Cornwall, Wales, Ireland and places across the Channel, and imported stones which were tougher than flint and so made better tools. From the Bronze Age, c. 1500-500 B.C., there are round barrows or tumuli, where important people were buried: they were usually cremated and their ashes put into large pottery urns. Bronze was used for valuable ornaments and the weapons of the leaders: flint was still in common use for weapons and tools.

The age of greatest activity was the Iron Age, c. 500 B.C.-400 A.D. The people, possibly of Celtic race, then inhabiting the Head, lived in round houses with central hearths. They fortified the Head on the landward side with double dykes so that, with water on the other three sides, it was a good defensive site. The double dykes are still there, though the banks have become lower and the ditches shallower with the passing of time. Pottery of many kinds was made by the Iron Age people and also imported by them, and there was a mint, from which thousands of Celtic British coins have been found, and a few

Roman ones, though the Romans do not seem to have lived at Hengistbury. The latest Roman coin found was of the Emperor Gallus, 351-354 A.D. The ironstone, which was abundant, was smelted and made into all sorts of practical and ornamental objects, and other occupations included farming, spinning, weaving and cloth-making, and probably some boat-building. Many relics of these various ages are in the Red House Museum, Christchurch, and there is also still the chance of an occasional find, as soil erosion brings previously buried objects to light.

The Saxon and Jute invaders who came after the Roman withdrawal did not fancy Hengistbury Head as a dwelling-place, but set up their own village, Tweoxneam (meaning "between the rivers"), later Twynham and finally Christchurch, and the Head was deserted. The name "Hengistbury" has no connection with Hengist: in Norman times the Head was granted to Christchurch Priory under the name of "Hednesburia", and it was sometimes called "Hinesbury".

Various schemes of improvement and fortification were tried during the centuries, but not much came of them. In the nineteenth century some open-cast iron-mining was carried out, and this left a large quarry, and nearly divided the headland in two, but was fortunately stopped. In 1929 Gordon Selfridge bought the Head, and planned to build a vast castellated mansion in the style of Carcassonne, but luckily this scheme came to nothing, and in 1930 Hengistbury Head was bought by Bournemouth Corporation, and has been saved from further depredations.

Besides its supreme interest as a Prehistoric site, Hengistbury is fascinating for its natural history. There are plants typical of saltings and sand-dunes, and of woodland, dry heath, wet heath and bog, all these being found in this small area. Nearly 250 species of plants have been found, as well as many varieties of sea-weeds, sponges, sea-anemones and other marine creatures. Numbers of different shells can be found on the shore, and over fifty kinds of fish and crabs and lobsters in the sea and the river by the Head. There are several butterflies and moths, though nothing very rare, various species of dragon-fly, half-a-dozen or more noticeable beetles, and an outsize grasshopper called the Great Green Bush-cricket. A hundred or more different birds have been identified, some living there and some passing through on their migrations, and with about twenty mammals, and five or six reptiles to be found, no naturalist on Hengistbury can have a dull moment.

Bournemouth and Poole are beyond the Solent in nearly all the maps, but as they follow Christchurch without a break, at least by road, it is very easy to take a look at them before leaving the district. The most remarkable fact about Bournemouth is that, less than two hundred years ago, it was practically non-existent. In a Christchurch Cartulary of 1407 "La Bournemowthe" is just mentioned, but it was simply the mouth of the Bourne stream. In the next century it was described as "a place very easy for the ennemy to land . . . being voyde of all inhabiting". It does not appear to have been much used by "ennemies", but in the seventeenth and eighteenth centuries it was considered a good, safe landing-place for contraband, and was freely used by smugglers, including a noted character called "Old Gulliver".

One of the first houses was a little inn, *The Tapps Arms* (later the *Tregonwell Arms*), built in 1809 in what is now Old Christchurch Road. In 1810 a Captain Tregonwell, who had come to know and like the district while on military service in Dorset, decided to build a house there. At first he considered Mudeford, but concluded that he preferred the mouth of the Bourne, and built his house where the *Exeter Hotel* now stands, in Exeter Road. Part of the house is incorporated in the hotel, and is marked by a plaque.

From that time the place grew up at almost incredible speed, and before the end of the century it was one of the largest and most popular seaside resorts in England. The beautiful views and the miles of golden sand were great attractions, and another was the pine-trees which, as some old guide-books said, exhaled an odour acknowledged to be beneficial to the lungs and bronchial tubes. Hundreds of charming villas were built among the pine-trees, so that the people might inhale this salubrious odour, and all the usual seaside amenities, piers, concert-halls, public gardens and magnificent shops were soon added. The many good, mainly Gothic Revival, churches included St Peter's, by Street, who designed the London Law Courts, and St Stephen's, by Pearson, architect of Truro Cathedral. Unfortunately nearly all the villas have now been demolished and replaced by modern buildings, including vast blocks of flats, but one remains in the Russell-Cotes Art Museum on the east cliff, formerly East Cliff Hall. The Chines, equivalent to the "Bunnies" between Milford and Highcliffe, narrow, tree-clad valleys leading down to the sea, form a very attractive features.

Bournemouth is noted for its music. It was the first resort to set up a permanent Municipal Orchestra, one of its most celebrated conductors being Sir Dan Godfrey. This has now become the world-famous Bournemouth Symphony Orchestra, and has had several conductors of international reputation.

Literary people connected with Bournemouth have included the Shelleys, who owned much of Boscombe, R. L. Stevenson, who wrote several of his books at a house near Alum Chine named Skerryvore which had to be demolished owing to war damage but is now a Memorial Garden, John Keble, Thomas Hardy and others.

There is no break in housing between Bournemouth and Poole, and they share a postal district, but Poole has a much older history, having received its first charter in 1248. It has been a port throughout the centuries, and in the

Middle Ages provided ships and men to fight against the French and Spaniards. Harry Page, a fifteenth century buccaneer, known to the French as "Arripay", continually harried the French and Spanish ships, and took a great many prizes, but eventually a joint expedition was fitted out against him, landed at Poole and plundered the town.

Later Poole, like Bournemouth, was much frequented by smugglers who once, in 1747, actually attacked the Customs House, and captured a large cargo of tea, then one of the chief contraband articles.

Poole has been tremendously enlarged and rebuilt of late years, but the Old Quay, and the area round it, are still charming. There are some very good buildings such as the Customs House, Harbour Office, Woolhouse, Old Town House and Guildhall, many pleasant old inns, the famous Poole Pottery, some picturesque almshouses, and some handsome merchants' houses from the eighteenth century, when there was a considerable trade with Newfoundland as well as other parts of the world. The church, St James, c. 1820, is typical Georgian.

Poole Harbour is beautiful, and a safe, sheltered place for learning to sail, for those who are not yet skilled enough to venture into the Solent. In the middle of the harbour is Brownsea Island, now a National Trust Nature Reserve, and noteworthy as the place where, in 1907, General Baden-Powell ran a camp for about twenty boys, and so started the world-wide Boy Scout Movement.

Brownsea Church (St Mary), built 1853-4, includes some interesting furnishings of earlier dates. Brownsea Castle was built as one of Henry VIII's defence works. Later, it was used as a private residence and was added to in various different styles. At present it is a holiday home for a large London company, and is not open to the public.

CHAPTER TEN

Crossing the Solent

A S HAS been said, it is possible that, in the far past, people could walk across the Solent, near Lepe, at low tide. It is possible, too, that Bronze Age men may have crossed in their coracles, and certainly Roman galleys must often have been seen, crossing from their various stations on the south coast of Hampshire to the Isle of Wight, but there were no regular commercial passages until the eighteenth century. The first sailing-boat "passage vessels" could sometimes cross from Southampton to Cowes in 2½ hours, but they could take as long as 7 hours under adverse conditions, and occasionally the passengers had to complete their journeys by rowing themselves ashore. These vessels included the *Mermaid* and the *Frederick*, between Southampton and Cowes, and the *Sons of Commerce* and the *Fox* between Portsmouth and Cowes.

The first steam vessel actually to be seen in the Solent was the steam-yacht *Thames*, which called at Portsmouth on a voyage from the Clyde to London. For a short time in 1817 a steamer, the *Britannia*, ran between Portsmouth and Ryde, but the first regular paddle-steamer service between Southampton and Cowes was set up in 1820, by George Ward of Northwood House, Cowes, with the *Prince of Coburg*, a wooden paddle-wheel steamer with three masts. The *Thames* also ran for a time on the Cowes-Portsmouth route. Fares on these vessels were between 1s. and 2s. 6d.

A steamer specially built for the Southampton-Cowes run was the *Medina*, which was launched in 1822. She had a very able and popular skipper, Captain Knight. As well as the regular crossings, she sometimes made round-the-island trips, and in 1823 made quite an adventurous crossing to the Channel Islands. Many other paddle-steamers were built, at Cowes, Southampton, Lymington, Fishbourne (in the Isle of Wight) and elsewhere, and a regular paddle-steamer service was maintained between Southampton-Cowes, Portsmouth-Ryde, Portsmouth-Fishbourne and Lymington-Cowes.

At Southampton, ships could only come alongside at the Town Quay near the Watergate, until the Royal Pier was built in 1833, and opened on 7th July by the Princess Victoria. As Queen, Victoria embarked again from the Royal Pier ten years later. On this occasion, it is related, the red carpets laid down along the pier were not quite long enough, and the Mayor and Aldermen, following the well-known example of Sir Walter Raleigh, laid down their crimson robes to fill up the gap. The Queen thoughtfully avoided treading on the white fur trimmings.

From 1817 until the 1840 the paddle-steamers were made of wood. The first iron paddle-steamer seems to have been the *Ruby*, 1840, on the Southampton-Cowes route, but wooden ones were still built as late as the 1860s. One iron paddler, the *Wonder*, had a remarkable turn of speed. She also weathered a fearful Channel storm in 1846, and the captain was rewarded with a handsome silver salver for bringing her safely through it.

As well as conveying the passengers and their luggage, and sometimes their carriages and servants, safely to the Isle of Wight, these vessels often had exciting adventures in saving people from wrecks. They also had their little troubles, such as dissatisfied passengers who complained of being charged 6d. for a glass of brandy, but on the whole they had a very long and successful career. One wooden paddler, the *Vectis*, was the first steamer built for the Southampton, Isle of Wight and South of England Royal Mail Steam Packet Company (known more briefly and conveniently as the Red Funnel Steamers). She was launched in 1866 and withdrawn only in 1910.

The suitably-named paddle steamer *Solent Queen*, 1889-1948, which ran on the Southampton-Cowes route and made excursions all over the Solent and adjacent waters. (*Photograph by courtesy of Bernard Cox, Paddle Steamer Preservation Society*)

The *Lord Elgin*, built as a pleasure steamer in 1875, was bought by the Red Funnel Line in 1909, ran for some time on the Southampton-Cowes crossing, later became a cargo steamer, and was finally disposed of in 1955. The last paddle steamer of the Red Funnels was the *Princess Elizabeth*, built as late as 1927 and finally sold out of service in 1959.

At various times a dozen or more steam packet companies, or steam navigation companies, were running on the Solent trips, and as well as doing the crossings from the mainland to the Isle of Wight, they made trips to Brighton, Falmouth, Liverpool, Scotland and the Channel Islands and the

Paddle steamers *Sandown* and *Ryde*, (now withdrawn from service), with two of the post-war diesel vessels of the Portsmouth-Ryde service, moored at Portsmouth Harbour.

Continent. The railway companies were allowed to run their own steamers following an Act of Parliament of 1862. The London and South Western Railway ran a line from about that time until 1965, after which it was given up by British Rail, and only later taken up again by other companies. One or two other companies, from Weymouth and Bournemouth, ran trips into the Solent, but these were excursion steamers rather than steam packets. The excursion steamers often carried "a full band of music", and they had dancing, fireworks, and excellent refreshments including champagne.

The Royal Family often enjoyed excursions, and on one occasion 142 members of the staff at Osborne, many of whom had never left the island before, ventured across in the *Ruby* from East Cowes to Southampton, and thence by train to visit the Great Exhibition at the Crystal Palace.

The Portsmouth and Ryde Steam Packet Company had many of its vessels named after members of the Royal Family. The Southsea and Isle of Wight Steam Ferry Company, which ran just from 1873 until 1876, had wooden screw steamers. The first iron ship to be built in one of the Solent yards, or indeed south of the Thames at all, was the Hythe Steam Ferry Company's *Forester*, built at Southampton.

As well as the passenger steamers, the paddle tugs were a great feature of the Solent. As early as 1820, the *Earl of Egremont* was used for towing barges, and several Solent steamers were used for towing even if they were not officially tugs. The first steam tug built for use in Southampton was the *John Lee*, 1846, and the first screw tug to enter Southampton's Inner Dock at its opening in 1851 was the *Mary*

One tug, the *Belmont*, had a curious adventure in 1854. She was towing the *Walter Hood*, but something went wrong and the *Walter Hood* rammed the *Belmont*, causing her to tip right over and to lose her mast and funnel. The crew were rescued and taken on board the *Walter Hood*, but then the

Calshot lightship.

Belmont suddenly righted herself, and sailed off down Southampton Water without any crew. She was captured by the crew of the Calshot lightship, and her own crew soon afterwards caught her up in a rowing boat. On another occasion, she was rammed and sunk while acting as an excursion steamer at the Spithead Naval Review. Passengers and crew were saved, and the *Belmont* herself was later salvaged and did several more years' useful work. In 1884 the tugs were all taken over by the Southampton, Isle of Wight and South of England Royal Mail Steam Packet Company Limited.

Besides packet boats and tugs, lifeboats, and later torpedo-boats and destroyers were built in the Solent yards, and Royal Yachts have formed a picturesque feature of Solent life for over two hundred years. King George III reviewed the Fleet at Portsmouth in 1775 from the Royal Yacht *Princess Augusta*. In those days, yachts were very grand, and in general were only used by Royalty, ambassadors or other Very Important People. Most of the yachts were ketch-rigged, though a few were rigged as three-masted ships.

The *Victoria and Albert I* was the first British Royal Yacht to be propelled by steam. Queen Victoria had seven Royal Yachts, a number only surpassed by Charles II who had seventeen. Her Royal Yachts were *Victoria and Albert I* (1849) of 1,034 tons; *Fairy* (1845) of 317 tons; *Elfin* (1849) of 98 tons; *Victoria and Albert II* (1855) of 2,470 tons; *Alberta* (1863) of 370 tons; *Osborne II* (1870) of 1,850 tons and *Victoria and Albert III* (1899) of 5,500 tons. All were steam yachts, *Fairy* and *Victoria and Albert III* were fitted with screw propellers and the remainder had paddle-wheels.

Modern crossings of the Solent can be made in under ten minutes from Portsmouth, and about twenty minutes from Southampton, in the hovercraft and hydrofoils, and this suits busy people, though far less picturesque and adventurous than the crossings in the early sailing boats.

CHAPTER ELEVEN

Isle of Wight—Needles to Yarmouth

A FEW years ago, having completed the tour of the north shore of the Solent and the interesting places just inland, one could have crossed to the Isle of Wight by paddle-steamer from Bournemouth on almost any summer day. Unfortunately, these paddlers no longer run though some small pleasure-craft still cross in fine summers. The nearest public sea transport is the Lymington-Yarmouth ferry.

The Isle of Wight has been called "The Garden Isle", "The Primrose Island" and other poetical names. Sir Walter Scott described it as "that beautiful island which he who has once seen never forgets, through whatever part of the world his future path may lead him." Its shape has been described, by various old writers, as a "trapezium" or an "irregular rhomboid", or as that of a flounder, with Bembridge Harbour as its open mouth, or a turbot. To people living round the Solent, it is just "The Island", and hardly needs further description nor commendation.

Briefly, however, it is about 23 miles from east to west, and about 13 miles from north to south. From the Needles at the most westerly point, right through to Culver Cliff in the east, there is a ridge of chalk downs, Brightstone Down, 702 feet, being the highest. To the south of the main ridge there are more downs, including St Boniface Down, 787 feet, the highest point in the island. Along the south coast there are some fine cliffs, interspersed by beautiful chines, some, such as Blackgang, having quite awe-inspiring bare rocks, and others, such as Shanklin, having rich vegetation and waterfalls. Another feature of this side of the island is the Undercliff: this was made by landslides, caused when the rock known as "blue slipper clay" became saturated with water, and the harder rocks above slipped down towards the sea. The Undercliff is very sheltered, and covered with almost tropical vegetation, which caused a nineteenth century writer to suggest adding "The English Madeira" to the island's other names.

The whole island is rich in delightful little seaside towns, charming villages, interesting old churches and beautiful old houses, and anyone staying by the Solent should certainly take time to visit the south of the island too. The northern half, sloping from the central ridge of chalk downs to the Solent, is less exotic in character. It is undulating, and much of it is well wooded.

Human life in the island is known to have existed at least from the Bronze Age, as there are tumuli of the date. It was occupied at various times by the Romans, who named it "Vectis" and left a wonderful villa at Brading, the Jutes, Saxons, Danes and Normans, and most of the people who conquered the mainland of Britain. Tostig, brother of King Harold, raided it just before the Norman Conquest.

Christianity is said to have been forced on to the inhabitants by King Wulphere of Mercia in the seventh century. Whether or not this was so, the Venerable Bede recorded that the island was the last part of Britain to be converted. One of its early missionaries was St Boniface, after whom the Down is named. He came originally from Devon, and ended his life as a martyr in Friesland, in c. 754. The island became part of the Diocese of Winchester in the eighth century, and remained in it until 1927, when it became part of the new Diocese of Portsmouth.

At the time of the Norman Conquest, there were already ten churches in the island. William FitzOsborne, a cousin of William the Conqueror who had made him Lord of the Island, granted six of these to the Monastery of Lire in Normandy. The Normans took over most of the property of the island. Later, the French frequently raided the island, but never quite succeeded in capturing it. The Black Death and the plague took their toll of the island, as of the mainland, and interfered with what had been a flourishing cloth trade, though this later recovered. Another island trade, which usually prospered, was that of smuggling, carried on most ingeniously for very many years.

The Spaniards intended to use the island as a base for conquering England, but the defeat of the Armada, not far from the island, in 1588, frustrated this plan. Early in the seventeenth century, when the islanders became nervous of further attacks by the French, they asked Parliament for help with their fortifications, but when some Highland soldiers were billeted in the island, they soon became very unpopular. Sir John Oglander, of the very well-known island family of Nunwell, near Brading, described them as "beinge as barbarous in nayture as ther cloathes", and accused them of "murders, rapes, robbereys and bourglaryes", and the islanders seem to have concluded that vague threats of French raids were preferable to the tangible presence of these defensive forces. Sir John presented a petition to King Charles I for their withdrawal. The king went over to the island to review them, and shortly afterwards they were withdrawn.

When the Civil War began the islanders, except for some of the larger landowners, were largely on the Parliamentary side, and there was very little fighting.

Agriculture, throughout these vicissitudes, was usually a flourishing occupation. Yachting and ship-building, for which the island is now so famous, have grown up largely in the last two centuries, although there was some ship-building in the time of Elizabeth I. As a holiday resort, the Isle of Wight began to come into favour early in the nineteenth century, and when Queen Victoria adopted Osborne House as her seaside residence, the popularity of the island increased phenomenally. Recently, the island has been declared officially "an area of outstanding natural beauty", so there is quite a hope that it may not be too much spoiled by building and industry.

At the most westerly point of the Isle of Wight and of the southern coast of the Solent is the Needles Lighthouse, 80 feet high. The first lighthouse in the island was built c. 1314 on St Catherine's Hill by Walter de Godeton as a penance, it is said, for receiving illegally wine salvaged from a wreck, this wine being the property of a monastery. This lighthouse was used until the Dissolution of the Monasteries, and still stands, though it is no longer used as a light. It is an octagonal tower with a conical roof, and is familiarly called "the Pepperpot". Another lighthouse, "the Mustardpot" was begun in the eighteenth century, but was not finished, as it was too high up to show any light at sea in foggy weather. The Needles Point was a much better site. The lighthouse there has a white light which shows for 14 miles, and a red light which shows for 9 miles, and a foghorn, locally known as "the Cow" which can be heard bellowing for many miles during a fog.

The name of The Needles is said to have come from one tall, slim pillar of chalk, about 120 feet high, sometimes known as "Lot's Wife", which fell suddenly, with a resounding noise heard for miles around, one day in 1764.

The Needles.

There remain three great chalk rocks, more like teeth than needles. "Lot's Wife" was between the first and second from the shore, and the first was formerly joined to the island by an archway. They can be seen best from the sea, and so can Scratchell's Bay, just east of the Needles, on the south side of the island, where there are magnificent chalk cliffs with natural arches and large caves. On the Solent side of the Needles, they can be seen very well from Alum Bay, or from the Downs just above.

Alum Bay, just east of the Needles on the Solent side, has been famous for hundreds of years for its coloured cliffs. These are made by different strata of Bagshot Sands which, in some upheaval in the distant past, have become nearly vertical instead of horizontal. These sands are white, grey, black, yellow, various shades of brown, red and even blue and, particularly when the evening sun is on them, they are a wonderful sight. They used to be made into fascinating pictures of island beauty spots, and other glass ornaments, such as little lighthouses, the colours being used very cleverly. There is a very steep, difficult path down to the beach, but there is now a chair-lift for people who cannot manage the scramble. In 1561 a warrant for working an alum mine was granted to Sir Richard Worsley, of Chale. This mine was worked for a very long time, and the name of the bay comes from it.

The coloured cliffs of Alum Bay. The chair-lift can be seen on the left.

At the top of the cliff there is a monument to mark the site of some of Marconi's wireless experiments in the early years of this century.

The grand stretch of downland eastward of the Needles is now National Trust property and is called Tennyson Down. There is a cross to the poet's memory at the highest point. From it there is a glorious view of the Solent, as

101

well as of the western half of the island, and of Bournemouth Bay, the Purbeck Hills and the English Channel to the westward. Tennyson bought Farringford House, near Freshwater, in 1853, soon after being made Poet Laureate. He loved the island, and used to walk on the Downs almost every day. Farringford House is partly "Strawberry Hill Gothic" and partly a little later. Tennyson lived there for many years, and among the poems that he wrote there were "Maud" and "The Idylls of the King".

A great many Victorian writers, painters, musicians, philosophers and worthies of all kinds visited him there. Jenny Lind, "The Swedish Nightingale" sang in his drawing-room: Garibaldi planted a tree in his garden. Julia Margaret Cameron, the pioneer woman photographer, who lived nearby, often photographed him, though he was not always pleased with her results. She was a remarkable woman, noted for her philanthropy as well as for her photography. Towards the end of his life, Tennyson was much troubled by gaping tourists, and left Farringford for Aldworth, near Haslemere, where he was less disturbed.

From Alum Bay there is a good walk, part of the island coastal path, through Headon Warren and down to Totland Bay, on to Colwell Bay, past Cliff End, the nearest point to the mainland, and thence to Yarmouth. After Yarmouth, however, the cliff path becomes impassable, and one has to turn inland to Cranmore before coming down on to the water again at Shalfleet on the Newtown Estuary. There is also a road, B3322, from Alum Bay through Totland, becoming A3054 near Colwell Bay, and going on through Yarmouth and Shalfleet to Parkhurst.

Totland Bay is approached by road as well as by footpath. It has a small pier and esplanade, and one can fish or bathe there, though the beach is of shingle. Above the bay there are low, pine-covered cliffs, and a path called the "Turf Walk". Totland village is a small shopping-centre. From Totland one could, instead of going on north to Colwell Bay, turn east and come to the village of Freshwater, and go from there to Yarmouth by the River Yar. Freshwater is partly a pretty old village, among trees, and the church, All Saints, was one of the six granted to the Abbey of Lire by FitzOsborne. It is now mainly Victorian, but the north doorway is Norman, moved from a different position in the old church. The nave arcades are transition, and there is a fourteenth century brass and some other interesting features. The tower is fifteenth century, supported on thirteenth century arches with corbels. Lady Tennyson and some other members of the family are buried in the churchyard.

Modern Freshwater has shops and other amenities, and is a good centre for walking, but families with children would probably prefer to go on from Totland Bay to Colwell Bay, which has very good sands and safe bathing and, at low tide, fascinating rock pools. North of the bay is Cliff End, opposite Hurst Castle.

North-east of Cliff End is Sconce Point, and between this and the mouth of the Wost Yar is Norton, now a suburb of Yarmouth. In the Fort Victoria Country Park at Norton are the remains of the nineteenth century Fort Victoria, built on the site of a former fort, Carey's Sconce. This was the point from which Charles I was taken to Hurst Castle. Norton is a pretty little place with a background of trees, and a safe, sandy beach.

The River Yar, which rises near Freshwater, nearly makes this western section of the Isle of Wight into another island. The way into Yarmouth from Norton is now over what was the Old Toll Bridge, but formerly fishermen used to ferry people across. Their charges were according to the passengers' social standing, a working man having to pay only a penny, and a gentleman sixpence. The ferrymen opposed the building of the bridge but could not finally prevent it. The toll was at first 6d. for a "car, hearse, litter, omnibus, stage coach or other like vehicles".

Yarmouth, though a small town, is one of the most historical in the island. It was mentioned in the Domesday Survey as "Ermud", and later became "Eremue" or "Eremuth". It was given its first charter by Baldwin de Redvers in 1135, and several kings later confirmed this charter. King John visited Yarmouth at least twice. A shipbuilder, John le Shepwricht, known to have been working at Yarmouth in 1297, is the earliest whose name has been recorded. The town was twice attacked and burnt down by the French, in 1377 and 1524, and for a time was reduced to about half a dozen houses, but in 1547 Henry VIII built one of his defensive castles there, after which the town gradually grew up again and became prosperous. The castle, which has been well preserved, has some round, brick-lined powder-magazines which served the guns on a platform above. It was built by George Mill at a cost of £1,000, a vast sum for those days. The north and west walls were protected by the sea, and south and west walls by a moat. There is a carving of the Royal Arms of Henry VIII over the east gate. In Queen Elizabeth I's time, the castle had twelve guns, and three gunners who were paid 6d. a day, but the garrison was increased when required. The castle was kept as a defensive work until the 1870s.

The *George Hotel*, which adjoins the castle, was the house of Sir Robert Holmes, Governor of the Island in King Charles II's time. Holmes had an adventurous career. He served under Prince Rupert in the Civil War, was exiled during the Commonwealth, joined the Navy at the Restoration and fought against the Dutch. He captured a Dutch ship with a cargo of gold off the Guinea coast, and the coins minted from this gold were the origin of the guinea in English coinage. He was also famous for helping to drive the Dutch out of "New Amsterdam" in North America, and renaming it "New York", in honour of the Duke of York, later James II. A fine statue of Sir Robert, on his monument in Yarmouth Church, is said to have been taken from a captured

Yarmouth Castle.

French ship. It was to have been a statue of Louis XIV but, as the head had not been completed, Holmes had it finished off with his own head. He was Governor of the Island from 1667 until his death in 1692, and he entertained Charles II in his house. As the *George Hotel*, it has been considerably modernised, but it still has a fine oak staircase and seventeenth century panelling.

St James' Church dates originally from about 1635. It was built partly by public subscription, the former church having been in ruins, and Yarmouth at that time going through one of its penurious periods. The tower was added in 1831. The Holmes Chapel, with its monument, is the most interesting feature. On St James' Day, 25th July, Yarmouth had special celebrations. On a pole, hung out from the old town hall, was a stuffed glove, looking like an open hand, and signifying that the authorities would be open-handed on that day, and would not pay much attention to small breaches of the law.

There are some pleasant old houses and cottages. The town hall, c. 1763, has an arched ground-floor which was formerly open, and was used at one time as a meat-market.

Yarmouth returned two Members of Parliament from the time of Edward I until the Reform Bill of 1832, although it seldom had more than a handful of voters, and at one time only two. Yarmouth Pier was built in 1876 and is 700 feet long. A tragedy occurred just off Yarmouth on 25th April 1908, when H.M.S. *Gladiator* collided, in a severe blizzard, with the American liner *St Paul*. 25 or more lives were lost in the naval vessel, and she had to be run on to the sand near Yarmouth beach, and later towed to Portsmouth to be broken up.

As a harbour, Yarmouth is as good as any in the Solent, as there is plenty of deep water in the Yar, by contrast to other harbours and creeks which are partly silted up and can only be approached cautiously at certain states of the tide. The Royal Solent Yacht Club has a very attractive club house dating from 1897, near the *George Hotel*, and there is a Yarmouth Sailing Club. At high tide, a dinghy can go right up the Yar, almost to Freshwater. The harbour, however, is often full: when it is, a red flag is shown during the day, and two red lights at night, at the seaward end of the ferry jetty.

Yarmouth has the West Wight's principal life-boat station. One was set up at Totland Bay in 1885, but Yarmouth is a much better launching-place, and the station was moved there in 1924.

Yarmouth Harbour. On the right is the Castle, and left, behind the masts of the fishing boat, is one of the large new ferry boats from Lymington.

CHAPTER TWELVE

Newtown to Carisbrooke

THE coastal path continues from Yarmouth, with occasional slight diversions inland, to Newtown Bay and beyond. Much of the Solent coast here is National Trust property. There is some pretty wooded country between Yarmouth and Newtown. The celebrated Regency architect, John Nash, had a house at Hamstead, about half a mile inland and west of Newtown Creek, as well as his more famous East Cowes Castle. Newtown, was, in fact, one of the oldest towns in the island, and at one time was an important port. The Danes are said to have landed there about the year 1000 A.D., but presumably at that time it cannot have been more than a small hamlet. The town was founded in 1256 by Bishop Aymer of Winchester, and was then called Francheville, meaning that it was a town free from manorial taxes. Like Yarmouth, it was raided by the French in 1377 and largely destroyed, and when it was rebuilt as Newtown it never regained its former importance, though it was another of those rotten boroughs returning two members to Parliament until the Reform Bill. Its most famous Member was John Churchill, later Duke of Marlborough.

The Town Hall at Newtown.

Some of the thirteenth century streets can be traced, running as parallel grass tracks between trees, but no really old buildings remain. The church, or Chapel of the Holy Ghost, was built by Livesay of Portsea in 1835, in good Early English style. There is a fascinating little Georgian town hall, now National Trust property, and some Georgian estate cottages, but in general Newtown is such a quiet, countrified place, that it is difficult to think of its ever having been one of the chief ports of the island.

Newtown Creek is one of the most fascinating of the Solent harbours, though it is considerably silted up, and has many shoals and sandbanks which make navigation difficult. It is, however, very popular with yachtsmen, but visitors should make arrangements with the harbour master to be sure of accommodation. In shape, the creek is rather like a jellyfish with long tentacles. Western Haven, Shalfleet Creek, Newtown River, Corf Lake, Causeway Lake, Spur Lake and Clamerkin Lake stretch out westward, southward and eastward. There are some facilities for yachtsmen at Lower Hamstead and at Shalfleet. In early times the creek was well known for its oyster-beds, probably patronised by the Romans when they were stationed at Carisbrooke, or in their villa at Brading. For some time the industry died down, but lately it has been revived in Newtown River and Clamerkin Lake, and is now very flourishing.

Newtown Creek.

In the middle of the creek is a 300-acre local Nature Reserve. This includes woodland, river, salt-marsh, tidal mud-flats and shingle banks, and is an admirable place for observing sea birds and other wild life. It has a warden and an observatory, and includes one of the island's Nature Trails. The Reserve was formed by the Isle of Wight Natural History and Archaeological Society, which was founded in 1919 and has done splendid work on conservation. Red squirrels may still be seen in the wooded parts of the island, and there is a rare plant, the Wood Calamint, and a rare butterfly, Glanville's Fritillary, found on the island and nowhere else in the British Isles. A few adders may be about in dry summers, but they usually keep out of the way of human beings, and only bite if provoked.

Shalfleet, which may be approached by road from Yarmouth as well as by pathway or by water up Newtown Creek, is a pretty village on the Caul Bourne, one of the streams leading into Newtown Harbour. It has a church with a low, square, very strong early Norman tower, evidently built for defence. The tower has a small north doorway, but originally had only a doorway leading into the church. The nave also has a Norman north doorway with a tympanum, possibly depicting Daniel in the lions' den. The south arcade and some excellent tracery in the south aisle date from c. 1270 and the chancel from a little later, and there is a good Jacobean pulpit.

The massive defensive tower of Shalfleet Church.

The village of Calbourne, about two miles south of Newtown Creek, has a row of charming old cottages called Winkle Street, beside the Caul Bourne. The church there is largely Victorian but has a partly thirteenth century chancel, and two interesting brasses, one fourteenth century, probably to William Montacute, Earl of Salisbury, and the other to Daniel Evance, a well-known preacher and Presbyterian Minister of the Commonwealth, c. 1652. There is also an old water-mill, open to the public during the summer.

About four miles east of Calbourne lies Carisbrooke Castle, one of the most famous buildings in the island. The poet Keats, who was staying near there when starting on his poem "Endymion" ("A thing of beauty is a joy forever"), writing to a friend, said that wherever he might go in the world, he supposed that he would never see a ruin to surpass Carisbrooke Castle. It is magnificently placed on a high bluff of downland. It was occupied by the Romans in late Roman times. Invading Saxons under the leadership of Cerdic and Cynric in 530 A.D. fought the men of the Isle of Wight and defeated them. The stone walled fort, now largely hidden by Norman earthworks, is said to be the scene of this battle.

The gateway of Carisbrooke Castle.

When William FitzOsborne, first Norman Lord of the island, died in 1071, his son Roger succeeded him, and held the post for seven years, but then rebelled against the King and forfeited his land. Carisbrooke Castle then remained in the hands of the king until 1100, when the Lordship was given to Richard de Redvers, who died in 1107, leaving the castle to his son Baldwin. During the Civil War between King Stephen and the Empress Maud, Baldwin sided with the Empress. Stephen besieged Baldwin in Carisbrooke Castle until the water supply ran out, and he was obliged to surrender. Stephen exiled him, but he was allowed to return in 1153, when he began building the keep. He died as Lord of the Isle of Wight in 1155. He was buried in Quarr Abbey, which was his own foundation.

The most notable of all the Lords of the Isle of Wight was Isabel, the widow of William de Fortibus, Earl of Albemarle. She was a great builder and was determined to strengthen the castle and make it absolutely impregnable. She was so successful in this that writers of the period describe the castle as "the new Castle of Carisbrooke". Isabel died in 1293 and the castle went back to the Crown, and remained in its possession until 1355, except for a short period in 1308-9, when it was held by Piers Gaveston, the favourite of Edward II of tragic memory. Richard II granted Carisbrooke and the Lordship of the Island to William de Montacute, Earl of Salisbury, who built the three-storey block of domestic buildings which adjoin the Great Hall. In 1377 the French, after their raids on Yarmouth and Newtown, proceeded to besiege Carisbrooke Castle, but failed to take it.

By the end of the fifteenth century, the Lordship of the Island had returned to the Crown, and only Captains of the Castle were appointed, their title being changed to that of Governor in 1582, and so remaining until 1944.

At the time of the agitation about the Spanish invasion, a seaman named Jacob Whidden went to the island and gave a very grave report of Spanish preparations which he had somehow witnessed. Sir George Carey, then the Governor, wrote to Sir Francis Walsingham, Elizabeth I's Foreign Minister, calling attention to this and stressing the need for further defences. The keep and curtain wall of Carisbrooke Castle were repaired and strengthened, and the castle, and every parish in the island, were given guns known as the "Carisbrooke Falcons", one of which is preserved in the Isle of Wight Museum. The defeat of the Spanish Armada, on 12th July 1588, removed this particular menace, but it was deemed expedient to strengthen the fortifications still further, and an engineer of great repute, Federigo Gianibelli, was given this work, which was accomplished between 1597 and 1600. Gianibelli had already designed the defences of Antwerp and of Berwick-upon-Tweed. His outer line of defences, completely surrounding Carisbrooke Castle, remains in fairly good condition to this day, and is of great interest as an example of the defensive works of the time.

Early in the Civil War the Earl of Portsmouth, Governor of the Island, was removed by order of Parliament. His wife was left holding the castle with a small force, and she courageously gave out that, if attacked, she would defend it against all comers rather than surrender it. The Mayor of Newport, a Puritan, declared that he would "fight the battle of the Lord" with the large force at his disposal. However, the Countess was persuaded to withdraw on honourable terms, so "the battle of the Lord" was never fought.

The chief event in the history of the castle during the Civil War was, of course, Charles I's imprisonment there. He was brought there on 3rd June 1647, from Place House, Titchfield. Colonel Robert Hammond, now the Governor of the Island, was a nephew of one of the King's chaplains at Hampton Court, and Charles believed that he could win Hammond over to his side. Had this plan succeeded, it would have been most advantageous to the King, giving him the island as a stepping-stone to the Continent, or as a base for attacks on the mainland. However, Hammond felt that, having been entrusted with the guardianship of the king's person by the Parliament, he must remain loyal to the Parliamentary side. As a reward for this loyalty, Parliament, as Sir John Oglander records, voted Hammond the sum of £1,000, an immense amount for those days, and an annuity of £500 for himself and his heirs.

At first, the King was given a good deal of freedom, and was allowed to send for his chaplains and servants. He went hunting with Hammond in Parkhurst Forest, and dined with some of the gentry in their homes. However, a strong guard was always mounted, as a precaution against his escape. One of the King's old servants, Harry Firebrace, managed to keep a most interesting journal, which has been brought up to date in modern times. Through Firebrace, the King was able to write to the Queen, the Prince of Wales, and many other friends. This faithful servant also tried to help the King to escape. He was to let himself down into the courtyard, where Firebrace would be waiting to conduct him over the Curtain Wall, beyond which horses would be in readiness to take him to the coast, whence a ship would take him to France. Unfortunately there was an iron bar across the window through which the King had hoped to climb out, and although he could put his head through the window, there was not room for his body.

Undeterred by this failure, the King decided to make another attempt to escape, on 20th May, two months later. This time the iron bar had been treated with nitric acid, and the attempt might have succeeded had not two sentries who had been bribed to "look the other way" decided that they must betray the plot to Hammond. At the appointed time the King looked out of his window, and saw several people obviously waiting for him, so he abandoned the scheme and never tried it again.

There was also an ill-timed rising in favour of the King led by Captain Burley, but this was instantly suppressed. This caused all the precautions to be considerably tightened, and the King was confined to the castle. His chief occupations were reading and playing bowls. Colonel Hammond had had a bowling-green made in the east bailey, and the King much enjoyed this recreation. He played with Hammond and the officers of the garrison, who included a Major Oliver Cromwell, a nephew of his great namesake.

Two of the King's children, the Princess Elizabeth, aged thirteen, and Henry, Duke of Gloucester, were with him at Carisbrooke. After his execution, they remained at the castle, but not long afterwards the Princess caught a chill, as a result of which she died. The little Duke was finally allowed to leave the castle and to join his mother and other members of the Royal family in Flanders.

On 6th September 1648 the King was removed to the Grammar School at Newport, his status being that of a prisoner on parole. He attended the sittings of the Commission which had been appointed by Parliament to negotiate with him, in the hope of being able to arrange a treaty, but unfortunately no agreement was reached.

After Charles's departure from Carisbrooke Castle, no outstanding historical events took place there. The last Governor of the Island was H.R.H. Princess Beatrice, the youngest daughter of Queen Victoria. She succeeded her husband, Prince Henry of Battenburg, as Governor in 1896, and died in 1944. After her death, what had been the Governor's residence became the Isle of Wight Museum.

The way into the castle is under an Elizabethan arch, and through the medieval gatehouse into the courtyard. St Nicholas Chapel, on the right, stands on the site of an older building. A church on the site is mentioned in the Domesday Book, and there was also one in the thirteenth century, of which there are a few remains. The present chapel dates from 1904-5 and is a memorial to King Charles. Opposite are the domestic buildings of the castle, consisting of the great hall, dating from the late twelfth century, the Chapel of St Peter, and some other rooms in which are now housed the Isle of Wight Museum containing, among other interesting exhibits, several personal relics of Charles I. A large Gothic-style window in the great chamber overlooking the courtyard is pointed out as the one through which Charles tried to make his escape.

Beyond these buildings is the Tudor well-house. The well itself was sunk in 1150, and supplied water to the castle for 750 years. It is 161 feet deep. It is worked by three donkeys, each of whom has an hour working and then two hours' rest time. They work within a great oak wheel, and walk 300 yards in order to raise one bucket of water. The shaft, round which the rope winds, is made of chestnut.

Beyond the well-house lies the keep, the ruins of which stand upon a huge artificial mound, made by William FitzOsborne. The keep was formerly higher than it is now and dates from c. 1335. There are various interesting features, including two fire-places back to back, a well 160 feet deep, possibly the original well of the castle, and formerly worked similarly to the other well, and a garderobe dating from the twelfth century, a great rarity.

From the vantage point of the keep there are beautiful views in all directions, notably over Carisbrooke village and the church with its very beautiful tower. This church was one of the ten already in the island at the time of the Norman Conquest, and one of the six granted by William FitzOsborne to the Benedictine Abbey of Lire in Normandy. The earliest works now existing are two small upper windows in the south wall of the nave. The south arcade dates from the latter half of the twelfth century, and the very handsome tower from the fifteenth century. There are some curious grotesques in the string-courses.

The chancel has been destroyed. It was formerly the church of a monastery founded in about the middle of the twelfth century. It was dissolved with other monastic establishments known as "alien priories" in 1414. During the sixteenth century, the property came by marriage into the hands of Sir Francis Walsingham, the famous Elizabethan statesman, who demolished the chancel and also the conventual buildings in order to save the cost of repairs. They formerly stood on the north side of the church.

The church contains a fine monument commemorating Lady Margaret, the second of the four wives of Sir Nicholas Wadham, a Governor of the Island. She was an aunt of Jane Seymour, third wife of Henry VIII. She is kneeling, and around her are the figures of poor people, two holding crutches, and all carrying a dole of food. Lady Margaret was renowned for her charitable works, and founded a hospital.

The remains of a Roman villa, with a good mosaic pavement, were discovered in the garden of Carisbrooke Vicarage, but not much of it is now to be seen. Anyone really interested in Roman remains must not fail to visit Brading, which, although about four miles south of the Solent, can be reached in a very short time from Carisbrooke, Newport or Ryde. It has beautiful pavements, the remains of twelve rooms and the hypocaust system, and all sorts of Roman relics, well preserved under cover. Many people consider it the best Roman villa in Great Britain.

CHAPTER THIRTEEN

Newport, River Medina and Cowes

ABOUT one mile to the north-east of Carisbrooke is Newport, the capital of the island. The town received a charter from Richard de Redvers during the reign of Henry II, and it was then that it became the New Port. It is a pleasant old town, the central parts of which are Georgian. It is situated at the highest navigable point of the River Medina. Its industries include timber and cement.

At the centre of the town is St James' Square. Here are the Guildhall (1819) by Nash and, down the High Street the Town Hall (1816) also by Nash: both are good classical buildings. A clock turret was added to the Guildhall to celebrate Queen Victoria's first Jubilee (1887). In the Market-place is a column, the islanders' memorial to Queen Victoria (1901).

Newport. The Guildhall (1819) and the Islanders' Memorial to Queen Victoria (1901). The lions on this monument have weathered to a remarkable shade of green.

The parish church of St Thomas is a handsome Victorian building in the Decorated style (1854-6). It contains various relics of the old church formerly on the site. The most notable monument in the present church is the very beautiful effigy commemorating Princess Elizabeth, the unfortunate daughter of Charles I. Queen Victoria was so saddened by the lack of any memorial that she commissioned Marochetti, a famous sculptor, to create one. The monument has a touching inscription, and the Princess, aged fifteen, is shown asleep, her face resting upon a Bible, while above are spikes, showing that she died a prisoner. There is a very fine Jacobean pulpit dated 1637, as well as several other features of interest.

Adjoining the church is a fine old house, dated 1701, known as "God's Providence House", since the house that formerly stood there was the only one whose inhabitants escaped the great plague of 1583-4. It has a large shell porch and a fine staircase, and is considered to be the finest house in Newport. Another interesting house, historically, is the old Grammar School where Charles I was lodged as a prisoner on parole during the sittings between him and the Parliamentary Commissioners.

From the eastern end of High Street, Quay Street leads down to the docks. This is the most picturesque part of the old town, and contains several delightful old brick warehouses. At the west (opposite) end of High Street are more old houses. No. 97 is a most gracious example of good eighteenth century brick work. The *Castle Inn*, dating from 1684, is said to be the island's oldest public house. In Pile Street is the Roman Catholic Church, a good brick classical building with a fine porch. Along the north side of the road from Carisbrooke to Newport runs a typical early Victorian terrace.

Quay Street, Newport. A study in excellent Georgian architecture marred by a late Victorian blight in the middle and a car park all the way along.

Charming old warehouses at the bottom of Quay Street, Newport.

Newport was the centre of the Isle of Wight railway system. The first railway in the island was that between Cowes and Newport, opened in 1862. After that, they spread all over the island, and the little steam locomotives puffed and panted up the severe gradients, pulling a motley collection of coaches, former mainland stock, some of them being discarded fourwheelers. Some of these interesting antiques found their way to various beaches, where they were used as bathing huts. True to tradition, the present coaching stock consists of old London Underground electric trains of equal antiquity. Whereas the old steam trains served all the more important places on the island, they have now all been scrapped. The only active line now is that starting from Ryde Pier, serving Brading and Sandown and terminating at Shanklin, a distance of seven miles. A section of the old track, about three miles long, has been preserved by the Wight Locomotive Society, and trips are run during the summer months from Haven Street to Wootton. On these trips one can easily return in spirit to the Victorian period, but Newport, once so important in the island railway system, is now only a centre for more modern road traffic.

Three distinguished men have represented Newport in Parliament. They were George Canning, the great Duke of Wellington, and Lord Palmerston.

116

Just south of Newport is the village of Shide. Princess Cicely Plantaganet, daughter of King Edward IV, and aunt and godmother of Henry VIII, lived there at East Standen Manor with her second husband, Sir John Kene or Kyme, and is said to have been happy there, after the brilliant but unhappy and worrying life of Court, mixed up with the politics of the time. She died there in 1507, and was buried at Quarr Abbey. Of her house, probably all that remains is a Tudor chimney, with a "Priest's Hole", or possibly smugglers' hold, leading off it. There is a picture of Princess Cicely in Carisbrooke Castle. The Earl of Southampton, Shakespeare's patron, occupied the house in the early seventeenth century, and part of it may date from his time. There is a well, reputed never to run dry, dating from before Tudor times.

Better remembered at Shide, probably, than the Princess Cicely, is Professor John Milne, familiarly known as "Earthquake Johnnie". He and his Japanese wife went to live, in 1895, at Shide Hill House, on the downs just above the pretty village of Shide. He had had a very adventurous career, travelling, surveying and mining. In 1875 he had been appointed Professor of Geology and Mining at Tokyo, and after an extremely hazardous journey overland via Siberia, Mongolia and China, and then by sea from Shanghai to Japan, had finally arrived on the day of a minor earthquake. This immediately aroused his interest in the subject of earthquakes and volcanic action. He started a Seismological Society in Japan, and did splendid work there in scientific study, and in its practical application to such matters as building sites and materials. He perfected a seismograph which could detect earthquakes anywhere in the world. After about twenty years in Japan, he came to the Isle of Wight and set up a seismological observatory at Shide. Scientists from all over the world visited him there, and also sent him all the information they could collect about earthquakes. His work was of immense value and though, of course, tremendous advances had been made since his time he is generally considered as "The Father of Modern Seismology". Unfortunately his house has not been well preserved. His grave is in St Paul's churchyard, Barton, near Newport.

The River Medina, which rises near Chale in the south of the island, at the foot of St Catherine's Down, widens out very much north of Newport, and is navigable up to Newport Docks at high tide. There is pretty, wooded scenery on both banks of the river, and there is a River Medina Nature Trail, which starts at Newport Quay, and includes salt-marches and interesting vegetable and bird life. Another Nature Trail, just west of the Medina, is in Parkhurst Forest, an old Crown Forest dating at least from Norman times. For people who find the works of man as fascinating as those of nature, the Albany Steam Museum lies just north-west of Newport and south of Parkhurst Forest, on the A3054 road.

The River Medina, south of Cowes.

About 1½ miles north of Newport is the Wight Marina, with berths for 300 yachts. On the road from Newport to Cowes, a little to the west of the Medina, is Northwood, which has an interesting old church of Transition date, with a rich south doorway and a Jacobean pulpit.

Cowes, divided by the Medina into East and West Cowes, is thought to have been a port in Roman times, doing some trade with the mainland. The remains of a small Roman villa were discovered there in 1864. The name "Cowes" is sometimes thought to be derived from a sandbank, formerly called "The Cowe", in the Solent nearby. Another suggestion is that, when Henry VIII built two of his defensive castles at East and West Cowes, a chronicler wrote "These forts will *cow* any Spanish or French enemie", and that this is the derivation of the name.

Shipbuilding had been carried on in the island from quite early times, and was certainly practised at Cowes in the reign of Elizabeth I, when a ship of the line was launched at Cowes in the year of the Spanish Armada, 1588. In the eighteenth century, frigates and three-decked ships of the line were built for the Royal Navy, and since then ship-building, sail-making and allied trades have become the chief industries of the island. Flying-boats were made during the two world wars and for a little while after the second one, but now

118

seem to have declined in importance. Hovercraft, however, are built at Cowes, and a small aeroplane, the Islander, is made a few miles away at Bembridge.

All along both banks of the Medina, there are fascinating ship-yards, sail-lofts, offices and marine stores. Sails for many of the most famous yachts have been made in Cowes. One of the most famous suits of sails was that made for the Royal Yacht *Britannia*: this required about 4,000 yards of 18-inch canvas. The best canvas was made of Egyptian cotton, but now canvas has been almost entirely replaced by Terylene. "Vectic" Terylene is exported all over the world, by millions of yards, as well as being used on British yachts.

Cowes began to be more of a residential town in the latter half of the eighteenth century. The High Street, which is narrow and winding, has some pleasant houses of that date, and there are others along the front. In 1795, the man who became the famous "Arnold of Rugby" was born at Westbourne House, a handsome red-brick porticoed house, not far from the Floating Bridge to East Cowes. His father was a Customs official at Cowes at that time. Later the family moved to East Cowes. Westbourne House has a plaque recording Arnold's birth, and there is also a plaque to his memory in St Mary's Church. This church was originally built c. 1655, but was completely rebuilt in 1867, except for the remarkable tower, described by some writers as Egyptian and by others as Grecian in style. This was built by John Nash in 1816, but is rather unlike his usual work. Near St Mary's Church, in Northwood Park, there is a fine and interesting house, Northwood House, probably designed by a pupil of John Nash, and dating originally from the early nineteenth century, with additions of c. 1840. It is now used as offices by the Cowes Urban District Council, and Northwood Park is a recreation ground, in which there are some rare trees.

For a time Cowes was a centre for sea-bathing, and old engravings show bathing-machines with "modesty hoods". These machines were drawn up and down the beach by capstans, instead of by horses. At the present time bathing is enjoyed more at Gurnard Bay, just west of Cowes, where there is better sand and purer water.

On Egypt Point, the most northerly point of the island, there is a lighthouse, with a white, flashing light visible for ten miles.

From the Parade and Princes Green there are splendid views of all that is going on in the Solent. Even when it is not Cowes Week, there is hardly a moment from early summer until late autumn when there are not ships and boats of every size and design coming and going.

The Royal Yacht Squadron Castle is probably the most famous building. It was formerly one of the Henry VIII defensive castles, and retains its old platform, on which are twenty-two brass guns, which are fired to start the races during Cowes Week, and also for Royal Salutes.

Splendid views of all that is going on in the Solent.

Yachts approaching Cowes from the Solent have to avoid rocks to the west, and the Shrape mudbank to the east, but everything is clearly marked.

The first yacht known in England was one presented to King Charles II by the Dutch, and described by the diarist Evelyn as "that curious piece". The name comes from "jagten", "to hunt", and implies a vessel built for speed. Charles II had 25 yachts, one of which was built in Portsmouth. There were races for fishing boats and pilot cutters in the eighteenth century, and a Cowes Regatta, in which naval vessels took part, was held in 1776: there is a picture of this, by Dominic Serres R.A., in the Royal Yacht Squadron Castle. From about 1810 there were races between private yachts, with heavy betting on the outcome. An "Isle of Wight Regatta" in 1814 was again mainly for fishing-boats, money for prizes being subscribed by what the newspapers called "persons of the first distinction". These distinguished people watched from their private yachts, and also held reviews, balls and other social activities.

The Yacht Club was founded in 1815, with the Hon. Charles Pelham, later Lord Yarborough, as the first Commodore. Members had to own a yacht of at least 10 tons, and to be of high social standing. There were 25 cutters, 3 yawls, 5 schooners, 2 brigs and one full-rigged ship in the first Yacht Club list, but these were used for reviews rather than racing. Some of the famous yachts were Mr Thomas Assheton-Smith's *Menai*, Lord Belfast's *Louisa*, built at Cowes, and Mr Joseph Weld's three Lymington-built cutters already mentioned. There was also an official yacht, the *Medina*, belonging to the Governor of the Island. She had been built in the reign of William III, and was said to be a connecting link between the ships painted by the Van de Veldes and the yachts of the R.Y.C. The aristocratic yachtsmen were very adventurous, and sailed on quite hazardous cruises in quite small yachts.

The Prince Regent joined the Club in 1817, and it became the Royal Yacht Club on his accession to the throne in 1820. William IV had it renamed the Royal Yacht Squadron in 1833. The Club presented a Gold Cup in 1826 for competition among its members. Yachts of any rig or tonnage could compete. The first race was won by Joseph Weld's *Arrow*. At first there were no rules about how many sails might be carried, but when Cowes presented two Town Cups, cutters were limited to three sails, mainsail, foresail and jib, and the races became fairer. Later, the yachts were divided more into different classes, and a handicapping system was gradually worked out.

George IV presented a Cup in 1827, and other Royalty who presented Cups were Queen Victoria, Edward VII as Prince of Wales, and the Emperor Napoleon III of France, who instituted the "Emperor's Cup Race" from the Nab Lighthouse to Cherbourg. In 1851 the 170-ton schooner, *America*, launched that year for John Stevens, Commodore of the New York Yacht Club, paid a visit to Britain and was hospitably received by the Royal Yacht Squadron. She took part, with great success, in some very sporting races. A

Cowes, Royal Yacht Squadron Castle is seen in the centre of this picture. It smacks vaguely of Scottish Baronial architecture while Osborne Court to the left is decidedly Palm Beach. Cowering beneath Osborne Court is a small example of indigenous Wight style.

Cup, presented by the Royal Yacht Squadron, for a race round the Isle of Wight and open to yachts of any nation, either cutters or schooners, was won by *America* herself, with a little 47-ton cutter, the *Aurora*, owned by Thomas Le Marchant, only just behind. This race was watched by the Royal family from the Royal Yacht, *Victoria and Albert*, off Alum Bay. The Cup went to America and became known as the America's Cup and from 1870 yachts from Britain, Canada and Australia have unsuccessfully challenged for it.

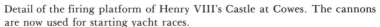

Detail of the firing platform of Henry VIII's Castle at Cowes. The cannons are now used for starting yacht races.

The Prince of Wales joined the R.Y.S. in 1876 and won one of the Town Cups with his schooner *Hildegarde*. He became Commodore in 1882, and it was largely his influence which caused Cowes Week to become so fashionable. The German Emperor also became a member, and his yacht *Meteor* had some exciting races against the Prince of Wales's famous *Britannia*. George V won many races with his *Britannia*, and the Royal tradition of interest in yachting has always been kept up.

All this racing led to many improvements in yacht designing, some of which have also been used for naval vessels.

Cowes Week is no longer so exclusive. Yachts of every nation, design, and size take part, and new designs, some for yachtsmen of quite moderate income, are introduced every year. Cowes Week is now so popular and the island so crowded that the best way to watch the races is to travel on some of the excursion steamers run by various companies for the occasion.

Many of the island-built yachts and other boats did splendid work in the two world wars. Earlier, some of them had been used for such good work as capturing slave ships, though many were used for smuggling and other less worthy objects. Whatever their uses, many of the most famous sailing-vessels of the world were built at Cowes and the other Solent ports.

East Cowes is largely industrial, but has its seaside resort section along the Esplanade. Hardly anything remains of Henry VIII's East Cowes Castle. John Nash built himself a magnificent Gothic castle at East Cowes, but most unfortunately, that also has been destroyed. Nash was buried in St James's churchyard, East Cowes.

CHAPTER FOURTEEN

Norris Castle to Whippingham

NOT far from where the old Henry VIII Castle stood is Norris Castle. This most remarkable pseudo-Norman stronghold is beautifully situated amid rolling park-land, with wide views over the Solent and Spithead. It was designed by James Wyatt for Lord Henry Seymour, and built between 1795 and 1805. It is said to be one of the very few untouched examples of Wyatt's work. It is especially valuable architecturally now that similar castles have been demolished at Steephill near Ventnor and East Cowes. By the main entrance are the farm buildings and stables. These were designed to resemble a great piece of city wall, fully embattled, with towers at intervals.

There were several Royal visits, including one from George IV before he became King. In the 1830s the Duchess of Kent, Queen Victoria's mother, rented Norris Castle, and the Princess Victoria, as she was then, had some very happy summers there, riding, playing by the sea, sailing in H.M.S. *Emerald*, lent to her by her uncle William IV, or just roaming about the park with a beloved cocker spaniel, Dash. She had only a very small room in the castle, leading out of her mother's, but in the park she had considerable freedom, perhaps more than she would enjoy at any other time of her life. She loved the place so much that she would have liked to purchase the castle when she became Queen, but this was not possible, so she bought Osborne instead.

The Duke of Bedford bought Norris Castle from the Seymours in the 1840s, and made various improvements in the sanitation and water supplies. Another Royal visitor to the castle was Kaiser Wilhelm, who stayed there when racing his yacht *Meteor* in the Solent. In his honour, a bath, described as "monumental" was installed, and also a shower, said to be dangerous as it showered mainly boiling water.

Cattle graze in bovine tranquillity beneath the ferociously fortified walls of Norris Castle stables.

 Norris Castle, in all its pseudo-Norman glory.

The house contains many artistic treasures, furniture, pictures and sculpture and other beautiful objects. It is still in private hands, but is open to the public on certain days in the summer.

Queen Victoria and the Prince Consort felt that they needed a quiet country house where they could relax; "a place of one's own, quiet and retired" to use the Queen's own words, and she was encouraged in this idea by Sir Robert Peel, one of her early Prime Ministers. Osborne House and estate were purchased in 1845. "It is impossible," she wrote, "to imagine a prettier spot—we have a charming beach quite to ourselves—we can walk anywhere without being followed or mobbed."

The old Georgian mansion, which stood upon the site of the present Osborne House, was much too small to accommodate all the Court, so a completely new house was decided upon. The house was in the Italian style, and was designed by the Prince Consort, assisted by Thomas Cubitt, a well-known London architect and builder, who had designed several squares and terraces there. It was built of fireproof material, a novelty in those days. The Prince probably chose the classical style as he was a great admirer of all things Italian. He was accustomed to compare the view across the Solent with the view across the Bay of Naples. Descending the hill upon which the house is built is a series of terraces, adorned with a fountain and statues in the Renaissance style. The Queen and the Prince laid the first stone of that part of the house called the Pavilion Wing, which they were to occupy themselves. It was finished in September 1846, and they went into residence. The additional accommodation for the staff was in the two eastern wings.

So began the glorious happiness of the Royal couple which, sad to relate, was only to last for fifteen years. Whenever they could possibly spare the time they went down to Osborne for a short break, except for the summer visit to Balmoral. They enjoyed this idyllic existence, and often wandered out in the evenings to hear the nightingales sing. The Queen, however, was too conscientious to relax entirely. As well as being Queen, she was the Squire of the villages round her estate, and she took an enormous interest in their welfare. She used to celebrate Christmas at Osborne, and this was observed in the traditional way, including a Christmas tree for the children of the estate.

The Royal party also came in summer for Cowes Week, and took a great interest in the yacht racing and all the activities of the Solent. They came more and more to love the district, and the dream palace they had built for themselves.

Even after the tragedy of the Prince's death at Windsor in 1861, his lonely widow continued to return to Osborne, which she kept exactly as it had been in his lifetime. One of her closest friends during this dark period was the ex-Empress Eugénie, widow of the Emperor Napoleon III of France. She had the same history of a long widowhood, as her husband died in 1873. They had lived in exile in England after his defeat at Sedan in the Franco-Prussian War. Eugénie lived on for many years, and died in 1920.

Queen Victoria still had some enjoyment from her life at Osborne. It is recorded that she sometimes breakfasted on the terrace, under a large umbrella, and was regaled with Highland music played by a band of pipers, so combining her two great loves, the island and the Highlands.

It was at Osborne that the Queen, surrounded by a vast number of relics of her dear one, died on 22nd January 1901. So closed the longest reign in English history.

As King Edward VII, Queen Victoria's eldest son, had no wish to live at Osborne, he gave it to the nation. The Household wing became a convalescent home for officers' and a part of the buildings and estate were for some years a Royal Naval Training College, where cadets went for two years between preparatory school and Dartmouth. Edward VIII as Prince of Wales, and George VI as Prince Albert, both did two years' training at Osborne.

At that time only a small part of Osborne House was open to the public, but Queen Elizabeth II allowed many more of the private and State apartments to be opened. The main body of the house surrounds an open courtyard, and there are three chief blocks, joined together by the Grand Corridor, which has a very handsome mosaic floor, and contains statues, pictures and cabinets of Victorian treasures. In the middle wing is the main suite of dining-room, drawing-room and billiard room. Prince Albert enjoyed a game of billiards, and he designed painted decorations for the billiard table. The private apartments of the Queen and Prince are on the first floor of this

 Osborne House, splendidly Italianate.

127

wing, and the Royal nurseries were on the second floor.

To the west of the courtyard is the "Durbar Room", a large reception hall decorated by Indian craftsmen in the Indian style, and containing many objects connected with the Queen's position as Empress of India, and wonderful presents given to her on the occasion of her Jubilee by her Indian subjects.

All the parts of the house open to the public form a magnificent museum of Victorian furniture, pictures, including the famous Winterhalter portraits, statuary, objets d'art and bric-a-brac, and several of the rooms have been left almost as they were when occupied by the Royal Family.

Prince Albert had also taken a great interest in forestry and landscape gardening, and he planted a vast number of trees of various kinds, oaks, elms and beeches, and some more exotic ones. In 1853 a typical Swiss chalet was sent over in sections, and re-erected in the grounds of Osborne. Here the Royal children were taught various useful accomplishments, the boys carpentry and gardening, and the girls the first principles of cookery. Here they could sometimes relax and enjoy themselves, and they often played host to their parents. The gardening implements were all hung up after use, and their owners' initials were clearly marked. One of the boys, the ten-year-old Prince Arthur, constructed, in 1860, a model fort made of bricks with earthwork fortifications and modern cannon, and named it "The Albert Barracks". He afterwards became Field-Marshal the Duke of Connaught. These interesting relics of the Royal children are on view to the public, as well as the contents of the house. The Queen's bathing machine is also shown, by the Swiss Cottage.

Whippingham Church is the parish church of Osborne. It is the fourth to be erected on the site, the first being Saxon, dedicated to St Mildred, thought to have been a Saxon princess. The only relic of this church is a sculptured stone of Saxon date, built into the exterior of the present south porch. This church was "Gothicised" by Nash in 1804. Dr Cox, the Victorian ecclesiologist, described it as being "rebuilt in Strawberry Hill pseudo-Gothick style", very much battlemented and pinnacled. It must have been of considerable interest architecturally, and it is rather sad that this, as well as Nash's East Cowes Castle, was completely demolished.

The present Whippingham Church was designed and erected by the Prince Consort, in conjunction with Albert Jenkins Humbert, a Southampton architect. In style it is a rich mixture of Norman and Early English. Dr Cox, who evidently had very definite opinions as to what a church should be, did not like this one, and described it as "both ordinary and pretentious". He even went so far as to say that "this strange fabric can hardly be considered suitable for divine worship", but Prince Albert had presumably felt like that about Nash's church.

Queen Victoria and the family worshipped there regularly. The Royal

Pew is situated in the south side of the chancel, and within it is a memorial to the Prince Consort, showing him with two angels holding a crown above his head. The inscription records that this memorial was "placed in the Church, erected under his direction, by his broken-hearted and devoted widow, Queen Victoria".

On the opposite side is the Battenberg Chapel, commemorating Prince Henry of Battenberg. He had married Princess Beatrice, Queen Victoria's youngest daughter, in the church. He died of fever in the Ashanti War of 1896.

A marble reredos of the Last Supper is a memorial to Queen Victoria, and the Sanctuary was, as an inscription states,
"enriched and beautified by her son, King Edward VII, and her other children and grandchildren
Her Children arise up and call her blessed"

The tower of Whippingham Church. An inspiration of Albert the Prince Consort, in, perhaps, one of his more Germanic moods.

CHAPTER FIFTEEN

Wootton to Ryde

SOUTH-EAST of Whippingham is the village of Wootton Bridge, which has been much modernised, but still has some pretty old houses. The church, St Edmund, has a beautiful enriched Norman south doorway, an Early English chancel and a Jacobean pulpit. The road from East Cowes to Ryde runs through Wootton Bridge, and the bridge itself crosses Wootton Creek, which is very pretty, with wooded shores, and is tidal up to the bridge. The harbour has been rather silted up and, like Cowes harbour, it has mud-flats to be avoided at the eastern approach, and some rocks at the western. Yachts can use it, but the water goes down quickly there when the tide is ebbing, and another hazard is that the best part of the channel is often taken by the Portsmouth vehicle-carrying ferry, which lands its passengers and cargo at Fishbourne.

The Royal Victorian Yacht Club and the Wootton Creek Sailing Club have their headquarters in Fishbourne Creek, and hold regattas in July and August.

George Brannon, the artist and engraver, from whose charming pictures so much is known of what the island was like in the first half of the nineteenth century, lived in Wootton. He published a book on "Vectis Scenery", containing pictures of the "Picturesque Beauties and places of particular interest in the Isle of Wight, drawn from nature and engraved by George Brannon" and also a topographical description, "Embracing," as he wrote, "every Information in the least degree useful to strangers". He had a large family, and several of his children died young and were buried in Wootton churchyard. Of the survivors at least two, Alfred and Philip, also took up engraving.

Philip, who moved in due course from the island to Southampton, was not only an engraver, but also an architect, and an inventor of airships, balloons, fireproof curtains for theatres, coloured gas-lighting for shops, fire-proof buildings, cottages with special health and sanitary features, methods of road and bridge-building and of preventing coast erosion, and other improvements too numerous to mention. Like Peterson of Sway, he was a pioneer of the use of re-inforced concrete. He also experimented with many forms of loud-speaker and systems of broadcasting, long before the days of wireless telegraphy. Many of his ideas have been incorporated into more modern inventions and some of his fire-proofing methods have been incorporated in St Paul's Cathedral. He found time, too, to write guide books, and to take a great interest in social work. While still quite young, he set up "Ragged Schools" for poor boys and girls in Newport, and himself taught the children drawing, etching and carving, leading on to other artistic and useful occupations. He was born in Wootton in 1815, and lived to be seventy-five: few men can have crammed so much work into one lifetime.

Wootton Rectory was known to be haunted, though by noises and lights rather than by a visible ghost. Another haunted house was a mill, from which the miller's daughter had eloped with a Spanish sailor. Returning some years later as a wealthy lady, she found that her father had committed suicide, and was overcome with remorse. She is said to have haunted the mill for many years, but mill and rectory have now both been pulled down, and new housing estates may well be discouraging to ghosts.

Between Wootton and Ryde is Quarr Abbey. This was founded by Baldwin de Redvers, at that time Lord of the Island, c. 1131. The name was taken from the nearby quarry, which had been in use since before the Norman Conquest. The Abbey was a daughter house of the Abbey of Savigny in Normandy, and was of the strict Cistercian Order, the emphasis being on poverty and hard manual work. It was the most important monastic house in

The great bulk of the Portsmouth-Fishbourne ferry wallows gently into Wootton Creek. Yachtsmen, beware, there are shallows on either side of it.

the island, and owned much property, manors, land, churches and mills, and had its own ships.

Baldwin de Redvers was buried there in 1156, and his wife and a young son, and several other notable people, including the Princess Cicely, were also buried there. There is some mystery as to the whereabouts of Princess Cicely's grave. Her coffin was said to have been made of gold, and it was thought that the monks had moved it and buried it again in a wood somewhere near the abbey, for fear that it should be stolen. A procession of ghostly monks, carrying a coffin, has been seen from time to time at nights by drivers along the road near the abbey. Indeed, the island seems rather a happy hunting-ground of ghosts, though modern holiday-makers are not often troubled by them.

At the Dissolution, Quarr Abbey was closed in July, 1536, and was sold to some Southampton merchants, who destroyed it almost entirely and used the material for other buildings, including the two Henry VIII castles at Cowes. Almost the only remains are some fragments of the abbot's kitchen or "cellarium", some thirteenth century walls, a fish-pond, and a barn possibly marking one side of the cloister. Some of the monks went to Beaulieu Abbey, but they must soon have been turned out of that too.

The modern Quarr Abbey dates from early in the twentieth century. French Benedictine monks from Solesmes came to the island in 1901, to escape from the anti-clerical French government, and a few years later one of them, Dom Paul Bellot, who had trained as an architect, designed the present abbey,

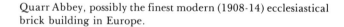

Quarr Abbey, possibly the finest modern (1908-14) ecclesiastical brick building in Europe.

Strength combined with tranquillity serve to make the interior of Quarr Abbey church perhaps even more impressive than its exterior.

which has been described as the finest modern ecclesiastical brick building in Europe. It was built between 1908 and 1914, of Belgian brick, rather in the Byzantine style. Local workmen did the actual building, under Dom Paul Bellot's direction. The church has a massive square tower, and a tall campanile rather like a minaret. The interior gives an impression of strength combined with lightness. The abbey grounds are surrounded by trees, and the whole place is a lovely oasis of peace in a too busy world.

133

The circular tour of the Solent could be concluded by crossing from Ryde to Portsmouth. The sea to the east of the ferry crossings is definitely marked on the maps as Spithead, not as the Solent.

For centuries, Ryde was a tiny village, with fishing and smuggling as its main occupations. It was known in Norman times as "La Riche" or "La Rye", but it can hardly have been rich at that time. It was destroyed by the French in the time of Richard II, but was gradually built up again. In 1782, when the tragic sinking of the *Royal George* took place, many of the corpses were washed up at Ryde, and were buried on the shore, not far from where there is now a children's boating lake.

In 1795, Ryde had a population of only 600, increased to 1,600 by 1811. In about 1812 a service of sloops between Portsmouth and Ryde was started, and by 1820 the population had risen to nearly 3,000. Landing at Ryde was, however, very difficult, and passengers often had to be carried ashore across the mud-flats. The building of the pier, begun c. 1813 and finished in 1824, did away with this difficulty. The pier is nearly half a mile long. Regular ferry services between Ryde and the mainland were opened up in 1826, and from that time the town grew and prospered tremendously, and now has a population of well over 23,000.

Many well-known and aristocratic people built houses there, and there are a great many superlative Victorian villas, as well as some in the Regency style. Very soon all the amenities of a seaside resort were added. Nature had already provided miles of beautiful and safe sands, and man added esplanades, concert halls, gardens, the children's boating lake, and everything that is necessary for a family sea-side holiday.

Ryde abounds in splendid villas . . . and also in less splendid or mutilated villas. The square bay windows on the one in the middle here make a horrid contrast with the gracious curves of an earlier generation. And the curse of the twentieth century, from Mini to Bentley, complete the ruin of the picture.

The main streets run quite steeply up hill from the front, and at the top is St James' Church, 1868-72, with a 180-feet spire dominating the view. It is considered one of the finest works of Sir Gilbert Scott. There are numerous other churches, of all denominations, nearly all built in Victorian times or a little earlier.

Typical Sir Gilbert Scott; the spire of St James' Church, Ryde, dominates the Ryde skyline with its sumptuous Victorian Early-English Decorated architecture.

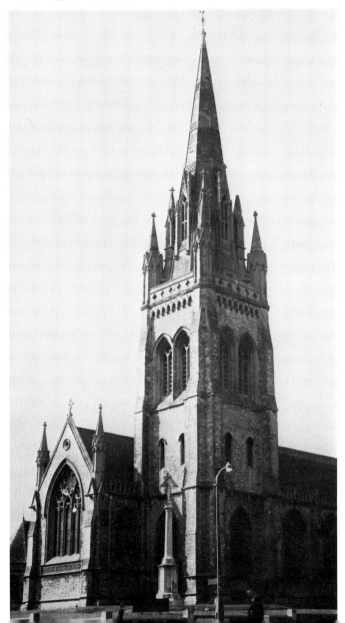

135

The pier was extended considerably at various times. The Tramway Pier, dating from about 1864, had at first horse-drawn tramcars, but about twenty years later the tramway was electrified. One very remarkable tramcar, believed to be Britain's oldest surviving one, is now thought to have been the fourth built for the Ryde Pier Company. It dates from about 1870, and is said to have been built specially for a visit by the Emperor Frederick of Germany and his wife, the Princess Royal, daughter of Queen Victoria, when they were Crown Prince and Princess of Germany. It was built locally, and very handsomely carved on its corner pillars with bunches of grapes and the initials R.P.C. by a Newport craftsman. It has windows of an ecclesiastical design, and is altogether a splendid specimen of a tramcar. It ran on Ryde Pier until 1936, being drawn in turn by horses, steam-engines, electric power and petrol engines. At the end of its career it was badly damaged in a collision, but it was taken by the Hull Transport Museum and completely restored. Although the museum suffered considerable war damage, the tramcar fortunately survived unhurt, and may still be seen there in all its glory.

The Railway Pier, constructed in 1879-80, had stations at both ends, and enabled passengers from the boats to transfer straight into the trains, either for Ryde itself or for its connections with all parts of the island. Now, as has been said, the trains from Ryde run only on one route, terminating at Shanklin, but Ryde is a good centre for all other forms of transport.

Like so many other Isle of Wight places, Ryde has its ghosts, and one is a little golden-haired girl, who was drowned when her father's fishing-boat overturned. She is said to appear sometimes to visitors, and to walk along the beach with them, crying, and showing an injured knee, but just before they reach the pier, she suddenly vanishes, leaving only a smell of seaweed. In general, however, Ryde is a very cheerful place and, for lovers of the Victorian, almost a paradise.

In 1901, the body of Queen Victoria, who had done so much to make the island famous and prosperous, was carried across the Solent to Portsmouth in her favourite yacht, the little paddle-steamer *Alberta*, escorted by ships of every navy in the world.

In 1977, the Solent and Spithead were once more thronged by vessels of all nations, on the joyful occasion of the Silver Jubilee of Queen Elizabeth II, who reviewed the fleets from the Royal Yacht, the present *Britannia*.

For pageantry and history, for occasions grave or gay, for work, play or adventure, there can hardly be, anywhere in the world, any stretch of water to surpass the few miles of the Solent.

Ryde is a cheerful place and architectural enthusiasts will be cheered by the nice little portico on the right in this view of Ryde.

A train putting out to sea. A scene from days of yore, when elderly steam engines still puffed along Ryde Pier. The trains which now serve Ryde Pier are electric; but it must be added that they are second-hand from London Underground's Central Line and are among the oldest vehicles operated by British Rail.

Bibliography

Non-Fiction
Journeys of Celia Fiennes, Ed. Christopher Morris.
Rural Rides, Cobbett.
Hampshire and the Isle of Wight, A. Temple Patterson
Portsmouth, A. Temple Patterson.
Southampton Through the Ages, Elsie Sandell.
The Beaulieu Record, H. Widnell.
Creeks and Harbours of the Solent, Adlard Coles.
Memorials of the Royal Yacht Squadron, Gest and Bolton.
Further Memorials of the Royal Yacht Squadron, J. B. Atkin.
Victoria R.I., Elizabeth Longford.

Fiction
Mansfield Park, Jane Austen.
Children of the New Forest, Captain Marryat.
The White Company, Conan Doyle.
Requiem for a Wren, Nevil Shute.

(The last, though fiction, gives a very vivid idea of the Naval activities in the Solent, especially round about the Beaulieu River, during the war).

*   *   *   *   *   *   *   *

Dressed overall and manned from stem to stern, the aircraft-carrier *Ark Royal* takes her place for the Silver Jubilee Review 1977. Perhaps a futile weapon in this hideous age of nuclear war, this vessel nevertheless carries the name of several proud predecessors which graced the waters of the Solent and the seas of all the world when Britannia ruled the waves.

Index

River Test

A 36

A 31

M 271

Eling

Ma

LYNDHURST

A 337

NEW

Beaulieu

FOREST

Buckle

A 31

BROCKENHURST

LYMINGTON

Woodside

A 338

A 35

Yarmouth

River Stour

River Avon

CHRISTCHURCH

Mudeford

Barton on Sea

Keyhaven

Hurst Castle

A 348

Milford on Sea

Norton

Colwell Bay

POOLE

BOURNEMOUTH

HENGISTBURY HEAD

Totland

Freshwate

Alum Bay

THE NEEDLES

TENNYSON DOWN

DURLSTON HEAD

THE SOLENT AND
SURROUNDINGS

Scale 1 : 250 000

ENGLISH CHANNEL